CLASSROOM TO NEWSROOM

Terry Murphy

CLASSROOM

TO NEWSROOM

*A Professional's Guide
to Newspaper Reporting and Writing*

BARNES & NOBLE BOOKS
A DIVISION OF HARPER & ROW, PUBLISHERS
New York, Cambridge, Philadelphia, San Francisco,
London, Mexico City, São Paulo, Sydney

To my wife, Joan Sue Murphy,
and my daughters, Kelly Brooke and Lynn Sue

Grateful acknowledgment is made for permission to reprint "Writing a Property Tax Story" by Gregor W. Pinney which appeared in the September 23, 1981 issue of the *Minneapolis Star and Tribune;* reprinted with permission from the *Minneapolis Star and Tribune.*

FIRST EDITION

Designer: C. Linda Dingler

Library of Congress Cataloging in Publication Data

Murphy, Terry, 1936–
    Classroom to newsroom.

    (Everyday handbook ; EH/586)
    1. Reporters and reporting.   I. Title.
PN4781.M83   1983   070.4'3'023   83–47596
ISBN 0–06–463586–4 (pbk.)

83 84 85 86 87 10 9 8 7 6 5 4 3 2 1

ACKNOWLEDGMENTS

Inspiration and insights that have helped me learn came from many, but with some the debts are greater:

The late Burton Marvin, dean of the William Allen White School of Journalism at the University of Kansas, helped get this once-failed student back into school. Once that miracle was achieved, professors Calder Pickett and Melvin Mencher provided lessons on ways to think that to this day help me learn.

The editors trained by the late John Harris demonstrated to me that timidity is not required to publish profitable small-town newspapers.

Bob Hoyt, a classmate at the University of Kansas and a friend, viewed the bare bones of an outline and saw that this book could be. Without his encouragement, the book would not exist. Edward Bassett, a Salem, Oregon, editor, and Warren Agee, a journalism educator at the University of Georgia, offered suggestions that made the book more coherent and useful. John Bremner of the University of Kansas saved me from my lapses of grammar.

My editor, Jeanne Flagg, invested the time and care required to understand what I was attempting with this book, and had the skills to improve it.

Ron Haxton, Harper & Row's college division representative in Minneapolis, provided valuable advice that guided my preparation of the manuscript.

CONTENTS

3 WRITING   50

4 SOURCES   65

5 ADVICE TO THE STRIVER
(Murphy's Almanac for Farming the Fourth Estate)   80

INTRODUCTION

The principal difference between a rookie reporter and a journeyman is experience. But experience is not the lone difference; some reporters lack the persistence and care to ever become journeymen.

The better journalism schools offer the liberal arts education and the training a beginning reporter needs. Some rookies can contribute at a high level very early. But to become a journeyman you must do the work of reporting. The purpose of this book is to ease the trip from classroom to newsroom and to help you excel.

Attitudes and awareness are discussed at least as much as techniques. There are some sermons mixed in that reveal my biases and passions. Murphy's laws are scattered throughout. It's all aimed at helping you develop a working philosophy that can serve throughout your career.

Some might say that these suggestions and philosophies are fine for big-city papers but they just won't work at papers with fewer resources. I disagree. Editors and reporters who can think and write clearly are the greatest resource any newspaper can have. Not all of them gather in large cities. If those qualities of the mind are combined with the energy and interest to get out into the community, you have most of the ingredients that contribute to a first-rate newspaper.

Schools can't and shouldn't train you according to the competitive circumstances of the paper you will work for. But the problems or strengths of a paper can make a great difference in what is expected of you.

Life generally will be easier if you work at a paper that is gaining circulation and advertising revenue. "Losers" will be working harder, trying to make the most of those things in life that come free: splashier page designs, brighter writing and an eye for scooping the opposition. If you land on a struggling paper, remember that shorthandedness does not relieve you of your obligations to know what you are reporting.

Most reporters would rather work for *The New York Times*, the *Washington Post* or perhaps the *Los Angeles Times* or the *Chicago Tribune*. These papers confer instant status as do a handful of others. Their traditions vary, but all deal from a solid power base. They are big; they deliver the readers who buy the goods and services that advertisers have to sell.

But whether you work at a newspaper where the approach is successful or at a newspaper where the editors are struggling, you need guidelines. This book provides some, not as rules that cover all circumstances, but instead as reference points you can cite as you try to find your way. They start with the assumptions that the best test of journalism is the service it renders the public and that the foundation of our democratic republic is an informed electorate.

Your part, after leaving the classroom, should be acquiring the skills of a journeyman and developing a professional working philosophy that can serve you throughout your career. I hope this book will help you.

The biggest problem you're likely to have isn't a lack of exciting things to cover or below-average pay scales. As the comic strip character Pogo says, "I have seen the enemy and it is us."

—*Terry Murphy*

1

YOUR OBLIGATIONS
AS A NEWS REPORTER/WRITER

Chances are that on your first day at work you will be assigned a desk, receive a short course on the telephone system and a longer course on the electronic news system. You will meet your supervisor, fill out employee records, receive an identification card and be told that there is a waiting list for a parking spot. At some point that nonsense ceases and you are given an assignment. You are now a working reporter, albeit a new one. Start thinking like a reporter.

LEAVING YOUR FINGERPRINTS

You will learn hundreds of things before you become a journeyman reporter, and most of them will take time and practice to master. Bosses realize that you will make mistakes, but they had best not be many, and certainly none that are caused by not caring. Along with a college degree and common sense, you are expected to bring a commitment to accuracy and fairness that is grounded in an awareness of how easy it is to get things wrong.

Names, ages, addresses, titles—all are facts that an editor has a right to expect even the rawest rookie to check and get right without having to be told. That means you check names, ages, addresses and titles yourself. You don't ask the reporter at the next desk how to spell something. You look it up yourself. Make it a habit.

An accomplished journeyman works with precision and thoroughness. That cannot be done if your primary focus is volume. Certainly, you need to be productive; but more important, you need to get it right. Your name goes on the copy and it is your job to vouch for the facts. Don't be sloppy, don't allow someone to stampede you and don't take a chance and turn in something you can't vouch for. Getting in trouble for being too slow is nothing compared to what happens when you don't get it right.

If you are concerned about the time it takes you to report and write your stories, start early, stay late, check and double-check. Skip lunch if you must. But be thorough and accurate. Be precise. Excuses are for losers and second-raters.

You cannot acquire a journeyman's skills simply by turning out bales of copy. Your progress should show in production, of course, but it must be production of quality.

UNDERSTAND THE ASSIGNMENT

A common problem between reporters and editors is the lack of a clear understanding as to the scope of the assignment, the length of the writing and when it is due. Don't let this be your problem.

Whatever the story, it is important that you, as a beginning reporter, have an understanding with your supervisor as to how much time can be devoted to it. If the supervisor has a different idea of how long it will take, you can have problems.

It is fundamental to succeeding that you learn to communicate easily and clearly with your bosses. If you work for someone who tends not to support your taking time to dig into things, approach *that* problem with specifics rather than a plea. Telling the supervisor specifically what must be checked and where you have to go will work better than saying, "I need more time."

Frequently, a story proves to be different from what an editor thought it would be. Keep your editor informed; don't let him be surprised when he reads the copy. If you run into a dead end, such as a source who won't cooperate, try to work it out on your own. But if you are stymied, ask your supervisor for suggestions.

If all that seems elemental and obvious, it is nonetheless important. Confusion on the first day can lead to mistakes that get you off to a poor start. Assuming you survive the first day, the first week and even the first month, the time will come when your suggestions for stories will be heard.

Some editors don't want suggestions from new reporters. Initially, that makes sense. But as you learn more of what is happening in the community, you should be developing your own story ideas.

You can learn a lot about what editors want by studying the cover pages of the sections your work appears in. The front page offers you a primer of your editors' news judgments. Read each story to gauge how many of the five traditional news values can be found. Use this checklist:

1. Timeliness—When did it happen? What is news today might not be news tomorrow.
2. Consequence—So what? So it happened; whom does it affect and how does it affect them?
3. Proximity—Where did it happen? Elsewhere, we might not report it; in our territory, we report it.
4. Human interest—Is it interesting? Many stories are news because they are funny or capture our interest.
5. Uniqueness—Is it unusual or is it so commonplace as not to be news?

Most stories contain several of those values. Three or more in one story give you a page-one contender. The worst editors lean heavily on timeliness, uniqueness and human interest in choosing their subjects. But whatever values are reflected by the display of stories, the front page can provide a practical guide for a beginning reporter.

If you work for a paper that emphasizes the serious business of city, county and state governments, your first challenge will be to understand your subject. Don't be satisfied just to report the actions taken by government officials. You need to find ways to tell the reader the consequences of those actions. Deadlines might make that impossible for reporting on the first cycle, but Sunday papers tend to provide the space and time needed for more detailed reporting.

Television and radio can beat you at reporting the surface details of a story, but you should not be at a disadvantage in helping readers understand what it means to them. Reporting things of importance to the readers in ways that provide compelling reading is one place where you can shine.

Start by finding subjects that affect many people. Then try to find a living person you can use to illustrate the details that enhance understanding. *The Wall Street Journal* is a good model; its reporters consistently find individuals whose stories illustrate important issues. You should be able to use your ideas in the reporting even if your editors pick all the subjects.

Deciding what to cover should involve both editor and reporter. A broad range of possibilities should be explored. The practices at most papers are far from this ideal. Consider how the process works at one large Midwest paper: The general assignment reporters line up at the editors' desks each morning to receive assignments. The reporters are not asked but rather they are told what they will do. The newspaper is, by the way, a good one.

The other extreme presents greater perils for beginning reporters. There, reporters do what they want, pretty much when and how they want. Virtually every newspaper has reporters who, for various reasons, have received free rein. If enough reporters hold that license, you have a reporters' paper.

But can there be a truly rational process for setting a reporter's agenda? Few things are totally anything. The worst newspapers are enslaved to the agendas of others—park board agendas, housing authority agendas, city council agendas, county commission agendas. Too often that approach defines news as being anything done by elected or appointed officials.

Public agendas deserve examination, but it is of limited value to report the workings of government unless this is done in a larger context. Doing nothing more than quoting officials and recording motions might fulfill someone's sense of duty, but it seldom helps the reader understand important issues and how they affect him or her.

One way to broaden your perspective is to view life as city planners often do. They organize activities under seven general headings to measure the quality of life:

Housing
Transportation
Public safety (police and fire protection)
Education
Health care
Jobs, economic health
Amenities (parks, recreation, the arts)

Use of those categories moves the focus of reporting closer to the concerns and experiences of the average citizen. City council members might know what they are doing, but unless the reporter explains the actions in a context that includes more than the agenda of any one meeting, the reader will have trouble understanding what's going on. For example:

A city council awards the cable television franchise without discussion. Considering that millions of dollars of profits are involved, it is likely that lots of maneuvering preceded the vote. If the council doesn't include discussion of those details on its agenda, does that mean the reporter has no duty to report it?

The example makes the point that not everything we need to report appears on official agendas or takes place in public meetings.

The narrower your view of what is fit fare to report, the more likely you are to produce a dull, predictable newspaper. (The city council meets every Thursday, so there will automatically be a council story in the Friday paper, whether or not anything newsworthy was done. That gives too much weight to timeliness in judging news.)

This is not to say that reporters (or editors) should be ignorant of government actions. Government officials hold enormous powers. The things politicians and bureaucrats do, and their rationale for doing them, need to be understood and reported. You can't do this if you aren't plugged in.

The question should be how to cover powerful institutions, not whether. Even the rawest rookie can appreciate that.

FINDING THE BETTER STORIES

If stories produced by reporters rank from zero to ten, it's fair to say that most newspapers concentrate on stories worth only fives or sixes, and seldom find time to report the nines and tens. This is a mistake. Nines and tens are a good trade for some sixes and sevens.

Here's an example of a nine or ten: In Minneapolis, police reporter Tom Davies took time to analyze what was happening in city politics. He used a form of journalistic arithmetic to give context to a series of scattered events that had made the police union into a decisive political influence.

The indications of the union's power had been reported separately: Aldermen made Minneapolis police among the best paid in the country. Aldermen approved police pensions but did not raise revenues to pay for them. Aldermen exempted police from accountability to a public board that heard all other civil rights complaints. One effect of the police union's power was that some officers felt free to break the vice laws they were supposed to enforce.

Most of this was known to the city hall insiders. They knew how things worked. But until Davies reported it in a cause-and-effect context, citizens could not comprehend how things worked in Minneapolis and how it affected them.

The police gained power in the dominant Democrat-Farmer-Labor Party because the liberal and conservative wings of the party were evenly balanced. That meant that several score of policemen could decide the winner in the primary elections by doing everything from lobbying fellow officers to passing out campaign literature on their own time. Their work was legal and they used their power to bargain with candidates. A mayor, who lost one election without police support and won another with it, acknowledged that their support made the difference.

In exchange, the campaigning police officers got to name the chief of police. That done, the chief gave key assignments within the department to other campaigning police. Meritorious work faded as a consideration.

Reform started after Davies reported how things worked and how political influence affected the department. The mayor chose not to seek reelection and the police chief resigned; a candidate who promised to take the police department out of politics was elected mayor.

David Phelps and Dennis Cassano reported on financial problems created by the political clout of the police and other powerful unions. Foremost among these, the city council increased pension benefits without thoroughly examining the long-term costs. In time, the Minnesota legislature modified public pension laws. The reform mayor reinstated merit as the basis of promotions and assignments within the police department.

The elements of those stories had been reported in bits and chunks, but the voters had no chance to understand the consequences until Davies, Phelps and Cassano put everything in context.

Davies devoted most of several months to his reporting. Cassano and Phelps worked full time for seven weeks. Such reporting is more difficult than passing along information handed out by public officials following a public agenda. Many reporters understand the trades and deals and the political climate in which they are made, but they lack the skills to report the facts without using anonymous sources. Frequently, not being able to get things on the record can be traced to the relationships reporters establish with sources. The chapter on sources offers advice for avoiding such pitfalls.

FINAL TESTS FOR STORY IDEAS

Unavoidably, reporters will do middling stories—some of which deserve to be reported. But you need to make time to identify the better stories such as Davies' police-and-politics reporting. Important as it is to report the more significant routine actions of government, editors and reporters should recognize how easy it is to become mesmerized by routine minutiae.

How can you tell a ten from a six or seven? You're on the track if the story, when written, offers perspectives that explain important events. While other reporters focus only on the rising costs of welfare, you can explain how the state welfare system was created and why, and who uses it and for what. A ten helps the reader understand how things came to pass and what they might mean for tomorrow. In reporting the stories, find case-history illustrations rather than quote bureaucrats.

If you are assigned to cover a beat, your story possibilities have already been refined. Some stories on a beat require no deep thought. The state needs to borrow several hundred million dollars to get through a tight month? Automatic story. But include the reasons why it needs to borrow money, and what would suffer if officials didn't act. And is this likely to happen again, or is it a freak, one-time event? How will the money be repaid and at what dollar cost? Don't just report that the interest rate is 11 percent. Include the dollars that will be paid as well as the percentage.

A good journalist provides the reader with enough background to make clear the implications of the problem and where it started. For instance, if the state must borrow to meet its payments to school districts, point out to what degree school districts rely on state aid. Talk to superintendents and report what they say the money is used for; ask how classroom activities would be affected if the aid were delayed. Such questions become obvious if you think in terms of who is affected and how. Too often reporters do not answer those important, basic questions.

In Minneapolis, the *Tribune* reported a cut in state funding by telling precisely what would change in two school districts—one of the state's poorest and in the largest district. The poor district eliminated field trips and delayed switching from outdated textbooks. The other borrowed money and reduced the number of school nurses.

In this case, serving the reader meant telling the story of reduced aid by reporting what happens in the classroom rather than stopping after quoting the state treasurer. The closer you get to the consumer's experience, the greater the chance your readers will recognize the importance of the story and read it.

Provide the details of the way things work, such as how one person succeeded in business. Avoid the clichés by digging for the specifics. It tells little to report that a restaurant succeeded by putting the customer first; that is a cliché. Telling readers that the owners spend lots of time training and supervising the help is better. Better still, tell the reader such things as the owner's decision to serve a more expensive coffee and use larger paper napkins—things the customer can enjoy.

Maintain a sense of history and do the research that will permit you to share that perspective with the readers. Some newspapers reported that Pleasant Colony lost the Belmont Stakes, the last race of the Triple Crown; the *Boston Globe* reported that he became the tenth horse to lose the Belmont after winning the Kentucky Derby and the Preakness. History and perspective—small touches provided by a thinking reporter.

Journalism texts admonish us to answer the questions *who, what, why, when, where* and *how.* (A surprising number of reporters fail to include all those elements.) To that list should be added: *What difference does it make? Whom does it affect?*

Most important stories affect human beings. Reporters should find some of those people to illustrate the effects.

Frequently, the first break on a story is big enough so that you can go with it and answer later the questions of whom it affects. The first break might be all the story is worth. Stories that fail to report the effects are usually little more than "inside baseball"—understandable only to those who are intimately involved.

There will be stories, however, that are very simple and often quite human. They, too, are worthy of reporting. *Blessed is the journalist who reports the bright, funny story.*

OUT IN THE WORLD

Remember—moderation in all things, including planning. Some deskbound types grab planning as an excuse to stay inside, away from the real world.

Planning need not confine anyone to an ivy-wrapped tower. To the contrary. Out to the streets, friends, face to face, close enough to smell—that's where it is. Go to the primary news sources. Know the differences between a primary and a secondary source. A primary source saw it; a primary source said it or heard it. Police reports of what happened are not primary sources—though the reporting officer might be if he or she saw what happened. *The further you are from primary sources, the greater the chance for getting it wrong.* For instance, there is but one correct way to spell a person's name. Ask the person. Phonetically, the name might be Jo Anne; the correct spelling could be any of several variations, including Joan. And don't ask how old someone is, ask his or her birth date. Age changes constantly; birth dates do not—except for persons of extreme vanity.

OUR REASON FOR BEING

Journalists should believe in publishing information, the same as scientists believe in basic research. You do it because it is your function in society; the Constitution protects it. Of course, if publication is to aid understanding, you must provide context. But once you have made it understandable, do what you can to get it published.

Keeping news out of the papers seems to be a growing practice. One area involves not reporting the identities of victims because it could add to their suffering.

Perhaps, but there is another side: Where the verified facts are not published, rumor is left unchallenged. Is the harm caused by rumor a lesser evil than that caused by publication? Why is the harm of rumor to be preferred? Concern for rape victims provides strong arguments against revealing their identities. There are special cases such as this. But remember, the journalist's basic function is to know and to tell—not to protect. When our readers are left ignorant on important matters, we have failed our job. We lose credibility if we suppress.

Often there is no *need* to tell. But such reasoning could keep from print much of what is in newspapers that make them useful and interesting. Let's not get too sophisticated. Almost always it is chore enough for a journalist to know and tell. Believe in that function. It is our reason for being.

And publication often serves the old and worthy right of the accused to face his or her accuser.

CAESAR'S WIFE AND ETHICS

Journalists need to do their work without fear or favor, and they need to be viewed by the public as being unentangled. To be above suspicion, choose your activities carefully and accept no gifts and few favors. But pronouncements of high ethics and canceled checks that prove you have paid your way are not guarantees of journalistic impartiality. When we review performances (and I include sports events), ethics are complicated further because we are delivering judgments born of taste and interest.

In Cincinnati, Eddie Halloran loved to inject this cautionary remark into discussions of ethics: "Does that mean that if someone tells me, 'Have a nice day,' I have to say, 'No, thanks'?" Those who seek absolute purity can find themselves taking odd stances.

I wonder about reporters and editors who go to elaborate lengths so their saintliness can be known and saluted. Their sense of virtue makes them hungry for opportunities to exhibit purity. It is as if their ethics are a battle flag rather than a commonsense guide.

Fairness is to be prized more than purity, though no reporter or editor should discount the need to remain independent. We should seek the ground where we can relax without causing our readers unnecessary suspicion. Most big-city papers seem beyond the heavy-handed influence of advertisers. So relax.

Prove your impartiality through the fullness and fairness of your reporting. Of course, if some lowlife makes a tainted offering, you should tell him, "No, thank you, and I hope you understand that I am offended by the suggestion." Leave no chance for misimpressions. Tell your supervisor of any such offer and make a record of the circumstances, including the time and place.

2

REPORTING

The best reporters go to see for themselves, to ask their own questions, to walk over the ground with their own feet. This isn't always possible, but it isn't coincidence that the better reporters find more reasons to go.

I have never heard anyone suggest that you could write a full profile without interviewing the person. How, then, can you expect to give a full account of what happened in a news story without going to the scene? Going converts the reporting from the abstract to the real. Two stories that follow illustrate the value of going.

The first involved a dinner club fire where people panicked. Those not killed by toxic fumes and heat were trampled. Only by going to the scene could the reporter understand such things as where the exits were in relation to the flames, and how wide the halls were. On the scene, the reporter could see if the hallways had fire sprinklers.

The other story involved a question of what rights developers received in exchange for providing land and helping finance a domed stadium. During negotiations for the rights, every reporter was frustrated by not being able to learn the details of the behind-the-scenes wheeling and dealing. Because of the secrecy, speculation was rank. Since those pushing the stadium were an integral part of the community power structure, suspicion was natural.

Perhaps frustration is what led one reporter to write that developers had been given *exclusive* development rights in exchange for the land and additional money. Whatever reasons he had for writing that, the contract stated otherwise. It gave the group *limited* rights to develop land around the stadium. By not reading the contract, the reporter made a serious mistake.

True, contracts are often dull and dry, confusing and obscure; it's easier to take someone's word than to check firsthand. You must not let laziness or the pressures of time keep you from checking.

Important, controversial reports should be based on research you can vouch for. Whether it requires traveling to a place or reading a document, every reporter should do his or her own research. Don't let someone else tell you what it states; you read it. Don't have someone describe something to you; go see it yourself.

Go. Check the story out. Talk to the people involved. It is called dealing with primary sources rather than secondary sources. Go to the scene. Knock on the door. Talk to the neighbors. Ask persons who work with the subject of inquiry. Call the parents, the grandparents, teachers, coaches—anyone who can give you information.

Many metropolitan newspapers are cursed with upstairs newsrooms. Reporters must go to the elevator or walk down the stairs to leave. Too many reporters are mesmerized by their desks. They cling to the telephone as their preferred instrument for communicating. (You can do plenty with a phone, but not everything.)

Some editors have driven reporters out of the newsroom, announcing loudly that there isn't any news in a newsroom. But before you go, know where to go and for what. Leaving the newsroom does not guarantee you'll find news.

Sooner or later, the better reporters go to the scene. Sometimes deadlines make that impossible, and some stories aren't worth it. But when you can't go, be acutely aware that you are reporting an abstraction. Ask your questions precisely and listen carefully. Make it clear in your story where you got the information, and do not leave the impression you were there if you weren't.

SOLID REPORTING REQUIRES TIME

Some reporters should be called conveyors. They send the reader whatever is handed to them. They would never think to challenge information. If a special interest group delivers propaganda in a speech or in a release, conveyors pass it along without context or challenge.

Some do business that way because they can't stand to put people on the spot. Others are too lazy or don't think of questions. Assigned a story in which two sides disagree, such "reporters" are content to pass along conflicting testimony without attempting to understand why the disputants disagree.

Reporting that attempts more than mere passing along of what is provided requires time. Analytical reporting is generally easier for the beat reporter who knows sources and has the background required to provide context that aids understanding.

But the general assignment reporter can do the same, even with a complicated subject, even starting from scratch. He just needs to remember how much there is to know and how easy it is to make errors of omission.

The first challenge in reporting a new subject is to find informed sources who will talk. But too much information and too many sources can be as big a problem as too little and too few. You need a sense of how much time a story might be worth. Any newsroom veteran can tell you how easy it is to waste time chasing promising leads that never develop into publishable stories. Staying on target requires solid news judgment.

It also requires knowing where and how to check information. For instance, a man who said he had been an undercover police informant went to the *Minneapolis Tribune* and said that a person who was working with him in writing an exposé of the police had been arrested on a phony charge. They had set him up.

That's exotic enough—if true. But converting a rumor of conspiracy into a report worthy of publication can lead to lots of dead ends. A common temptation is to sit down and listen to all the gory details—to play detective. Most of us enjoy an occasional touch of intrigue. In the instance above, we first sent a reporter to the police agency that would have had jurisdiction. No charges had been filed. That simplified the decision to scratch the effort.

If you want editors to give you time to pursue harder-to-get stories, you must be able to judge the validity of a tip. No newspaper can afford many dead-end investigations. Good reporters can dig through records and interview people. Very early you must determine what you need in order to publish. If you can't get something solid at the outset, put the story on a back burner or kill it.

But most questions of how much time should be spent have nothing to do with intrigue. Most often the question involves how much time can be justified in understanding a complicated subject. Here are some guides:

First, set the scope of the story: Write down the main points of focus. Stick close to those points and be wary of diversions. Consult with your supervisor before leaving the agreed-upon course.

Make the distinction between a story that takes a temperature and one that would provide a complete physical. Each can be useful and honorable, though good papers have editors who do not trust quick hits. Yet gathering information for its own

sake can ruin any newspaper if the practice becomes a governing tradition. Remember Murphy's favorite law: *A good journalist is someone who knows, who understands and who tells—in a
timely fashion.*

If you start from scratch on a complicated story, you need
support and time. Given that, there is no reason you cannot
provide authoritative reporting. But be leery of quick hits.

There might be reasons, such as competition, for you to report an investigation before all parts of the story are written. If
such is the case, be certain you have virtually all the reporting
done before the first piece is published. The furor of publication can scare sources away and cause records to disappear.
*Investigations and series should, as a rule, be completely written
and edited before the first article appears.*

And do not miss opportunities to follow stories. Any subject
worth a front-page story most likely could be of interest again.
Use a tickler file every day.

What's a tickler file? It's a series of thirty-one numbered
folders, one for every day of the month. You put stories you
want to follow in the appropriate folder. At the end of each day
you check to see what is coming up the following day.

Some people use a desk calendar for the same purpose. They
tuck clips into the calendar pages (the messy way) or write
themselves notes in advance. A tickler file is more efficient.

The advice I'm giving presumes that you and your editors
value authoritative reporting and are willing to invest the time
and do the work required.

There are papers where thoroughness is not valued. These
folks deal mostly with celebrities, authors and others who want
to use the paper.

But even stories such as those can benefit from a reporter's
talents. A Miss America toured campuses in the late 1950s, and
most newspapers published heart-warming accounts of her
dream come true, complete with a set of clichés to permit the
reader to disengage the brain. But one young woman reporter

looked at the beauty queen's résumé and saw that she claimed to be a member of the sorority the reporter belonged to. Thinking it odd that the sorority would not have trumpeted a sister's triumph as Miss America, the reporter checked with national headquarters and discovered a fraud. It produced a story that had the lead, "She's lovely, but is she ours?"

Any reporter, but especially the general assignment reporter, can approach work believing there is insufficient time to do a decent job. Thus convinced, such a reporter will go bumping along, taking what is presented. If you don't have time to prepare by reading clips, you can at least listen closely and ask obvious questions.

If you want to be a passive reporter—a conveyor rather than a challenger—you will find excuses for doing such kiss-off work. Many editors won't bother to kick it back.

Nor will there be challenges for stories taken from the freaks and geeks beat—those half-baked stories that focus on odd behavior: the family that travels the state fair circuit selling items on the midway, or the Siamese twins in the sideshow. Those stories belong in newspapers because they can reveal the human condition. But a conscientious reporter should be content to leave them to the feature-oriented word-fancier.

What is being urged on you is this: Learn to take command of a story—do the research required to be an authority of sorts. Use the reporter's skills so that you understand what you are reporting rather than just passing it along. Accept responsibility for checking things out. Understanding, truly understanding, will permit you to put complicated and complex stories into a context that gives the readers the information they need to judge things for themselves.

BALANCE AND FAIRNESS

There are two sides to every story, the old saying tells us. The idea is correct but the saying is literally true only when we describe two-dimensional objects. Life is more complicated. In addition to two sides, there is the top and bottom, not to mention the weight and color, in addition to hot and cold.

For a report to be fair, all parties must be given a chance to be not just heard but understood. (Yes, there's that word again—*understood*.)

In reporting a controversy, you should, if you can, present all sides at one time in a coherent context. Otherwise it is unlikely the reader would understand.

Balancing a story to make it fair should be viewed as more than an act of physics. Reporters who understand a subject are less likely to settle for stacking skimmed facts at opposite ends of a journalistic teeter board. They recognize that fairness is owed to the readers rather than the sources. Balancing distorted versions does not serve readers.

A common challenge to provide balance comes in reporting labor disputes. If management says it is offering wages that add up to 11 percent increases and the union says they are only 9 percent, you need to be able to take the base figures and check them yourself and show the reader how you did it.

On the workaday level, fairness requires that you start early in trying to reach people and be inventive as well as persistent. A halfhearted effort is unprofessional. The worse the light a person is cast in, the more you should strive to reach that person for comment.

A common problem comes on Fridays, when people frequently leave early for the weekend. Remember that the successful reporter goes forth, knocks on doors. On a rainy day, one is tempted to be a desk rat. But push away from the phone when it has failed to provide what is needed, and go down the stairs in search of what is missing.

A side note: If sources knowing you are trying to reach them *and* knowing what you want to ask about still decline to respond, the obligation lessens. But even then, they should be informed if the story will cast them in a bad light. So if by 1:30

P.M. on a Friday a person you need to talk with has not returned your calls, get in your car or start walking; reach that person's office or home.

If you wait until four or four-thirty, chances are you will not make contact.

Balance in a story involves the structure of the story as well as its content. It is not good enough to run the allegations in the top half of the story and then run a denial on a page inside. Responses to accusations should appear no later than the fourth paragraph. They should be more than perfunctory. Nothing stops you from finding a way to put a response in the lead sentence: "Alderman John Crop was accused Monday of tampering with a grand jury witness, an allegation he said was untrue."

Do not, however, permit the denial to run before the accusation as in "Alderman John Crop denied allegations . . ." If the allegations are worthy of publication, state the allegations first rather than open with a denial of something unfamiliar to the reader.

When reporting civil lawsuits, call the defendant. It is rare in civil cases that the first filing of court documents would include contentions from both sides. Few defendants will comment when reached, but call them anyway.

Not having a response adds to your burden to be fair. Remember the point of view from which a story is being reported and make it clear to the reader that completeness is missing.

Point of view can be very powerful in any story. Recently, the Immigration and Naturalization Service tipped the *Minneapolis Star and Tribune* that agents were going to raid several restaurants at which, they had been informed, aliens were working illegally. We were invited to join the raid.

I objected for two reasons. First, to accompany police officials on a raid would place us, the press, in a position other than that of neutral observer. Second, while a raid might provide drama that we could not get otherwise, participation was not essential to understanding the questions raised by aliens working without legal permission.

The better story would have been to find out who hired the aliens and ask whether they had done it before. If it is a crime to work without a permit, it is not a badge of honor to hire illegal aliens.

And in cities not contiguous to the border, it would be worth learning how the aliens got there. In Minneapolis, for example, several Japanese and Filipinos were arrested. How they got to the United States should have been reported. It seemed likely the assistance of others was required. It might have been worth learning if certain restaurants or other businesses are notorious for hiring illegal aliens. A reporter should learn how the system works and who is responsible.

Yes, doing that story the right way takes more time, energy and brains than are required to join police on a raid. But balanced and fair reporting often requires such efforts.

And while offering sermonettes, I suggest you keep in mind the sad joke about the quick and easy reporter, who is first with the story, exclusive with the retraction.

Urgency belongs in journalism. But we have higher obligations than to be first. Being fair, full and accurate are three.

OTHER PEOPLE'S STORIES

Sooner or later you will face the problem of what you should do when your competition breaks a hot local story. When it involves an investigation or allegations of wrongdoing, it is tempting to try to take the edge off the competition's story by publishing information that tends to discredit the first report.

For certain, check it out. But resist taking the cheap shot. Do not become a warrior in *la guerre urine* (*urinaire* to be precise). Have a little class; admire and respect enterprise.

It is possible to start late and work hard enough to take a story away from the competition. This involves pulling out the stops. Not only must you catch up, you also have to do the work to pull ahead. It can be done—sometimes.

And there might be instances where you can absolutely, positively, beyond any doubt, prove that the competition's report is, in its substance and its thrust, inaccurate. When that's the case, you have an obligation to set the record straight. But either prove beyond doubt that the report is unfair or inaccurate or leave the work of others alone. Don't nibble at the edges and don't niggle. No clarifications and no refinements. You go for the whole hog or you stay out of the barnyard.

Do not provide a forum for those who want to discredit the competition's report. Be content to build your own journalistic house. Do not tear down work done by others.

PRIVATE LIVES OF PUBLIC PEOPLE

John Kennedy is reputed to have been the eagerest skirt-chaser in the White House since Warren Harding caught Nan in a closet; John's brother Teddy has had problems driving. JFK's story might be considered entertaining; Teddy's could not be.

Publishing the story involving the death of Mary Jo Kopechne was never in question. She drowned in a car driven by Teddy Kennedy when it fell from a bridge into a tidal basin near Chappaquiddick in County Duke in 1969. A life had been lost and the circumstances raised questions about a public figure trying to duck responsibility.

But there will be less clear-cut questions involving the private lives of public figures. When does an action become the public's business? "When the action becomes part of a public record" is the answer for many editors. Accidents are clearly part of the public domain. So are padded expense accounts that show a public figure taking a friend on trips at public expense. That is fair game for print.

But what about John F. Kennedy? If reporters knew that the

president, a married man, was consorting sexually with others, should they have reported it?

Consider the choice made in 1863 by Sylvanus Cadwallader, a correspondent for the *Chicago Times*. In one day, Ulysses S. Grant lost 3,200 men in a futile attempt to storm the Confederate battlements at Vicksburg. The general did a time-honored thing—he got drunk and stayed drunk on board the steamer *Diligent* on the Mississippi on June 6 and 7. Grant's drinking already had raised doubts in Washington and if word had reached Secretary of War Stanton and President Lincoln, he could have been removed from command. Cadwallader saved the story for his memoirs, published posthumously in 1955. Grant won the siege, won the war and went on to become one of our worst presidents—thanks, perhaps, to the decision by one reporter not to report.

The question of when and what to report about a public figure's private life begs for a surfacing of personal values. It also offers an excuse for me to slip in a sermonette.

Reporters have a public trust. Thanks to improved pay, there is less likelihood a reporter will take out-and-out bribes. Concern for ethics has led some newspapers to impose stringent rules on gifts and favors. The concerns of these editors make them want from reporters and editors what Caesar wanted of his wife—that they be above suspicion.

The clearest and harshest rule is that we take nothing, not even free admission to events that we report or review. Most big-city papers pay the air fare for their reporters when they travel to political events or with sports teams. (Some papers have blanched, however, at paying the going rate of $500 or more for a ringside seat to report a heavyweight championship fight.)

But what about the ethical questions posed by the power of a president or a governor to literally "make" a reporter by granting access? A public figure who is willing to use access in that manner is a peril to the ethics of a reporter. Remembering that it is a journalist's job to know and to tell, you should gain access however you can. Right? It's a fascinating question and one that most reporters would love to have to answer, but might also fear to answer.

The reluctance to report the sexual wanderings of public officials can sometimes be traced to the sexual wanderings of the reporters themselves. It is aggravated by the star status of the television reporters, even those on the second string. (Not that they alone cruise, nor that all choose to.) Handsome or beautiful faces recognized by literally millions lead to cocktail party temptations for reporters. With the decision to wander comes a reluctance to report such activities by others. Whatever choices you might make, remember this: *To mix work with play invites peril.*

The question of what is public, and thus fair game to report, and what is private will never be answered to the satisfaction of everyone. But remember that a journalist is paid to know and then tell.

I suggest that you skip gossip, but don't run from news that walks the border between public and private.

Editors and reporters find more and more reasons not to publish information. Fear of lawsuits is part of the reluctance, and so is a misbegotten desire to protect the sensibilities of the public.

There are good reasons for caution and the application of taste. But newspapers exist to inform the public. Reporters are hired to serve the readers. The public can handle it and in fact require it. The "it" is information. Newspapers should publish "it."

SO WHAT? AND WHOM DOES IT AFFECT?

The value of asking "So what?" and "Whom does it affect?" was illustrated in the checking out of a report that there was a new way to reduce the spread of Dutch elm disease.

The method involved killing diseased trees with a herbicide injection. The dead trees attracted the disease-carrying elm bark beetles by providing a desirable place in which to burrow and lay their eggs. Later, when the herbicide dried out the host trees, it killed beetles, eggs and larvae. The dead, dried trees, no longer suitable for other breeding beetles, could be left standing or removed. In the park where it was tested, it reduced the number of trees infected by Dutch elm disease by 30 percent.

The combination of elements was one that almost always excites newspaper editors: a scientific breakthrough in solving a public problem. It wasn't up there with preventing polio, but it could help save trees.

But it became much less of a story when the question was asked:"So what? Who is going to be affected?"

The news value of the breakthrough faded when a few more questions were raised—such as how much it would cost. Probing revealed that it was too expensive to be used by the government. Nor did anyone expect private citizens to spend their own money to kill a dying tree in the hope of saving the trees next door.

So here was a piece of scientific news that faded when it was taken from the laboratory and placed in the real world. Many stories change when you ask how the public is affected. Always ask basic questions.

A caution here: Sometimes reporters make the mistake of thinking that they are to report only those events that they are assigned to. Such was the reporter who covered a basketball game but did not mention that police were called to arrest fans who were brawling in the stands. He was there to report basketball.

Life does not always follow the announced agenda. Without fail, report what everyone will be talking about as they leave the event— whether it be the fistfight, the naked streaker or the fact that the

council meeting was cut short due to a failure of the air condition-
ing. Remember to put it in context; not every oddity belongs in the
lead.

INFORMED SPECULATION

There will be times when you and your editors decide that you
want to report something *before* it happens. Now we are talking
about putting your neck on the line based on what sources say
is going to happen.

Before you do it, be careful.

Better yet, be double careful, and cautious too. Think of it as
jumping from roof to roof across narrow but high spaces. Done
right, it brings attention. A slip can be messy.

But it is fun to raise a periscope now and then to see where
the great ships of state are headed, instead of waiting for an-
nouncements that they have docked.

While reporting government, you can find yourself sub-
merged in the netherworld of politics, councils, legislatures
and such. Committees meet, charts and tables become like
spots before your eyes, and before you know it, you are march-
ing to the drum of chairmen, experts and governors. Some reporting of that sort is unavoidable.

But now and again you can get the jump by looking ahead—
anticipating what is coming up on agendas. Often all that's required is the thought, such as telling the reader what is likely
to happen to the property tax bill. That would require, in Minneapolis, knowing the mill rates for city, county and schools,
and minor taxing authorities such as transit and mosquito control. (Don't laugh; in Minnesota the mosquitoes collect nearly
as much blood as the Red Cross.)

By looking ahead and doing your own research, you can report ahead of those who wait for officials to appear before television cameras. But whenever you use informed speculation,

level with the readers and tell them what you're doing.

The most common occasion for reporting informed speculation occurs with political appointments. When to go with it and
when to wait will always be a matter of judgment. Whatever
you do, when proposing such a report, make it clear to your
supervising editor what the speculation is based on.

REPORTING POLITICS

To report politics, you need the journeyman's skills and the
historian's knowledge, not to mention an appetite for long
hours spent at places far removed from home. All the public
issues come together on this beat. Try reporting politics without sufficient background and experience, and you can count
on a fair measure of embarrassment—if you are smart enough
to know what you've missed.

The core of politics is partisan advocacy. Remaining wary of
partisanship is essential to being full and fair in your reporting.
Political parties are the backbone that keep legislatures erect
and working. Even in times of so-called one-issue politics, politicians must work in blocs to get done what they want done.
Those who stay completely outside "the system" get nothing
done. Legislative achievers find areas of mutual support. On
some votes, politicians rise to statesmanship, casting aside narrower considerations to do what they think will best serve the
entire public. But most of the time they think they best serve
the public by staying aligned with similar thinking people.

Too many reporters covering politics do not comprehend
that other forces influence votes by legislators, such as when
Southern Democrats vote with Republicans, or rural legislators
join metropolitan legislators in a vote. The proper starting
place for reporting votes or initiatives is the issue itself. First,
understand (there's that word again) how a proposal affects

people and then see how the partisan alignments hold.

Partisanship is important, but too many reporters try to explain everything in terms of party alignments.

Those who are elected serve the interests of the people who elected them—their constituents. Start your reporting by understanding where different factions line up on an important issue. Most voting blocs have changing memberships; the core of the group stays, but others shift in and out as their needs and consciences dictate.

A reporter can become confused inside the whirlwind of legislative activities. Committees and subcommittees meet continually. The differences between motion and progress can become blurred. The preventive for confusion is geared to two exercises: One, before the session starts, define the most important issues; and two, during the session, consult with the working leaders on where those issues are going.

And be reluctant to report process stories. A committee's approval of a proposal might mean that passage is assured or it might mean absolutely nothing. Ask the leaders. What's between this bill and passage? A stenographer can report committee actions. It takes a seasoned reporter to understand what the actions mean.

It is absolutely essential that reporters not permit politicians (or anyone else) to use the newspaper to present things in less than a full, clear light. That requires judgments by the reporter; they cannot be avoided.

For example, be alert to the old dodges that school boards and superintendents trot out when they need voter approval to spend more money. Generally, that story opens with the statement that the district will have to curtail or kill the high school football or basketball program, or maybe the band. Another favored threat is that unless the voters go for more spending, class sizes will increase dramatically.

It would be irresponsible to report dire predictions without noting that a vote is pending. And check to see if similar predictions were made in the past and whether the sky fell as forecast.

Most newspapers reserve politics reporting for the more experienced and enterprising of their staff. One reason is that politics is a beat on which it is absolutely essential that you cultivate reliable sources. It requires that you know the interests of your sources and filter what they provide through that awareness.

You need several years of experience of dealing with sources before trying to work politics reporting—the fastest reporting track in journalism.

MATH SKILLS

If a bureaucrat or a politician says that black is white, you are likely to feel comfortable challenging the contention. But can you confidently judge between a mayor's announcement that taxes will increase 11 percent and a citizens council statement that the correct figure is 16 percent?

A journalist, need you be told, is someone who knows. Sometimes, to know requires that you be able to figure percentages; you need to be able to start with a mill rate and figure for the reader the tax bills for a range of houses of differing assessed valuations.

You can't be a total math dummy and do that sort of work. And just as you can learn to write by using words, you can learn to figure by understanding mathematics. It doesn't require calculus or trigonometry or even algebra. Simple multiplication, addition, subtraction and division will get you where you need to go. Finished college and still can't do math? Consider night school. It won't hurt. Or there might be someone in the office who could teach you. Whatever, don't fake it.

Learn to figure a tax bill for houses representing typical values without having to rely on the city or county clerk. Some commonly used terms:

Mills: as in a mill rate of 36.53 levied against each thousand dollars of assessed valuation.

Fair market value or market value: generally a figure reflecting what the property would sell for. Prices paid for comparable houses are often used to set value.

Assessed value: the value assigned to property for purposes of taxing. Often based on a percentage of market value.

Property tax: the amount owed. It is determined by multiplying the mill levy (e.g., 36.53) times the assessed value.

Classes of property: Some places charge commercial and industrial property different tax rates. Often it is done by giving the homeowner a "homestead" credit which can be subtracted from the bill.

Taxes due: Most property taxes are paid in arrears. That means the tax levied one year is collected the next—generally in two equal payments, six months apart. Commonly referred to as first-half and second-half taxes.

Levy limit: Many states limit certain taxes in exchange for state aid.

Tax penalty: assessed for paying late. Generally a percentage added and/or interest charged on money due.

Tax sale: property sold to settle unpaid tax bills. Rarely does valuable property get sold this way, because the mortgage holder will step in.

Equity: the difference between the selling price of a property and what is owed on it. For example, if you own an $85,000 house and the mortgage is $50,000, your equity is $35,000.

Remember that property taxes can be deducted from income taxes, state and federal. Property taxes are criticized because the value of a home frequently does not reflect the owner's ability to pay taxes. Older people whose home values increased through inflation are often cited as being unfairly taxed because of this. Taxes not based on ability to pay are called regressive; those reflecting ability to pay are called progressive.

It is useful to remember the old saw that figures don't lie but liars often figure.

On page 35, there is a model story that uses informed speculation in reporting the things that can influence a tax bill. It can be done when a reporter understands material rather than just knows it. It's about the same as going into a final exam well prepared as opposed to having to rely on last-minute cramming.

Some of the more common stories reported in newspapers involve negotiations to write contracts between public bodies and their employees. Several warning flags should be kept flying during coverage of such efforts.

First, it must be recognized that a member of the Newspaper Guild or any other union has an unavoidable conflict of interest. Some might argue that this should disqualify a reporter. I disagree. Parents and taxpayers have an interest in the same negotiations, and being a union member, taxpayer and parent, I can tell you that my familial feelings have always outweighed my urges as a unionist. (My feelings as a taxpayer are muddled. Life in this country is still a bargain, but so much money is wasted that I hate to make the admission within hearing of government officials.)

The reporter's concern should be with sifting the figures offered by the two sides so that readers have a chance to judge the financial outcome. *It is not enough to report that the two sides disagree, and then present to the reader the points of disagreement. The reporter and editor must make sense of it for the reader by checking out what each side claims is true.*

Salary negotiation stories have several common sticking points, such as: the increase in salary for the "average" employee; and the percentage increase for the people at the low end of the pay scale and for those at the high end.

A common formula for figuring the average increase in salary is to total, for example, what the teachers' raises will cost the district and divide the cost by the number of teachers. But that formula can produce different figures if used by different people who start with different assumptions, such as how many full-time employees there are. If you get stuck with irreconcilable differences, try this:

Give the reader the number of teachers counted by the board members and tell how they figured the salary increase. Do the same with the figures provided by the teachers.

Use identical formats for presenting the disputed averages, such as: "The teachers' union arrived at the average pay by dividing . . ." The rule is to give the readers the base numbers (in the example that would be the number of teachers and the total increase), and explain the way they were used (multiplied or divided) as well as the product (the average salary).

Do not let both sides provide just the averages. Give the reader the base figures and tell them how each side used them in figuring. To do otherwise subjects the reader to a game of mathematical Ping-Pong.

You must understand the figures for yourself. It is not enough to provide a report that is but a superficial balancing of unexamined opinions.

The same obligation applies in reporting any disagreement. The laziest reporters focus on the dispute rather than sifting the charges and countercharges and making an investigation or assessment that will provide insights. A reporter should provide the information that will allow readers to understand the circumstances and judge for themselves.

When reporting numbers, always place them in perspective. A newspaper reported that 94 percent of a union's members voted to strike. It did not say whether that was 94 percent of six thousand workers or six dozen. There's a difference. The same story reported that workers were "demanding" an hourly increase of $2.50. It should have included the present pay levels, the date and amount of the last increase and the percentage of increase that $2.50 an hour represents. Do the arithmetic for the reader. Always include the whole, base numbers along with the averages and percentages. (And "demanding" is a cliché in most labor stories. Could it have been written that they were "seeking"? There is a difference in tone, and the story did not give other indications that the workers were strident. Do not stereotype your reporting by using clichés.)

FIGURING A PROPERTY TAX BILL

Few assignments strike more fear and dread in the hearts of young reporters than being told to write a tax story. Here is a checklist of the information needed to explain property tax levies:

1. Locate the agency that bills the taxpayers and collects the money.
2. Get the list of bodies with authority to levy taxes.
3. Create a table comparing the levies for this year, last year, five years before that:

Agency	Mills (1981)	Mills (1980)	Mills (1975)
County	57.14	57.04	53.47
City	31.02	34.27	41.12
Transit	3.43	3.43	3.43
Sewer, paving	6.16	6.16	5.78
Parks	11.27	11.27	14.85
Schools	43.41	43.27	55.67
Mosquito control	.09	.09	1.07
Total levy	152.52	155.53	175.39

4. From the assessor, learn the two or three most common valuations for houses being taxed.
5. Figure several typical property tax bills by multiplying the mill levy total by the two or three most common valuations.

6. Tell the reader when the bill must be paid and where the
   money can be sent.

WRITING A PROPERTY TAX STORY

There is no preferred format for reporting property taxes. But
the story that follows does a good job of providing the basics,
including doing all the arithmetic for the reader. It also shows
that you don't have to wait for all the bills to come in before
writing.

By Gregor W. Pinney
Staff Writer

The average homeowner in Minneapolis will probably find property taxes increasing by slightly more than 20 percent next year, wiping
out all of the relief that homeowners received last year and part of the
relief of the previous year. But the tax bill still will remain substantial-
ly below what it was three years ago.

The shape of next year's taxes came into clearer focus Tuesday
when the city school board adopted a tax levy that is only one-half mill
larger than last year's rate, rather than several mills larger as had been
expected. That means that the overall tax rate will go up only slightly
over last year's 103.116 mills if the city and county governments
achieve their goal of keeping the same rate as last year.

The exact rate will not be known until the levies are set by the city
council and the county board and by several minor taxing authorities
for such things as transit and mosquito control.

The average homesteaded property, which has a market value of
$58,036 on the city assessor's records, will be taxed at about $525,
compared with $436 last year, when the property had a value of
$52,124.

Even though the tax rate will not go up much, the taxes will increase considerably because of two factors: the increased value of the
property and the decreasing relief from various tax formulas.

A more modest house, which would get a better break from the
formulas, would not get such a steep tax increase. For example, a

house with a market value of $40,000 last year and $44,520 this year would have a tax increase from $315 to $356. That is 13 percent more, nearly all of which is explained by the 11.3 percent increase in the property value.

And in the higher brackets, in which homeowners have been getting a proportionately meager break from the formulas all along, the increase won't be so severe. The person who owned a $100,000 house last year that has inflated to a $111,300 house this year will pay $2,077 in taxes instead of the previous $1,761, an increase of 17.9 percent.

Another factor in all of these increases is that the state government has backed off somewhat in its support of local government and has shifted some of the burden to local taxpayers. That reverses the previous trend, in which the state assumed more of the burden and thus lowered local taxes.

The average house in Minneapolis in 1979, for example, had a market value of $35,200 and was taxed at $657. That dropped to $482 the next year even though the market value had gone up. It dropped further to $436 in 1981. Now it will go up to about $530.

The school board yesterday set its levy at 38.443 mills compared with 37.892 that property owners are paying this year. The new levy will be collected in May and October of 1982 and will be used for the 1982–83 school year. The school levy constitutes about 37 percent of the total city tax bill.

The small increase came as a surprise because various actions by the state legislature have tended to increase school levies by several mills. The basic "maintenance" levy, for example, has been set at 23 mills instead of the previous 21. But school officials found that they had enough money in several of their allied accounts, such as debt redemption and capital outlay, so they cut those levies back. And they once again won legal battles with the state assessors who thought Minneapolis was worth more than local officials thought it was. That brought in some additional money.

The fact that the average property owner's taxes will go up slightly more than 20 percent means he or she will get the benefit of a new state relief formula. The state has agreed to pick up three-fourths of any increase over 20 percent so long as it does not cost the state more than $200 in any one case.

In this case, it will cost the state only about $5, and the benefit will lower the homeowner's bill only from $530 to $525. So instead of suffering a 21.6 percent increase in taxes, the homeowner will get a 20.4 percent increase.

INTERVIEWING

When it comes to getting information, you can observe, use records, or listen to people. It is virtually unknown that you can get what you need from people without asking questions. The dictionary says the interview is a meeting for obtaining information by questioning a person or persons.

Naturally, you should be prepared to understand what you are hearing. You cannot walk in cold and do the same job you could if you prepared. As Pulitzer Prize winner Jim Polk puts it, "you get lucky by going through the monotony" of preparing and checking. He discovered, for example, that one of the children in Jonestown, Guyana, had declined an offer to go home. He did so because Jim Jones, the founder and leader of the religious colony, was the only person who had helped him. It was mentioned as an afterthought by a court employee while Polk was checking the circumstances surrounding court appointments of Jones as guardian of numerous youngsters.

As Polk listened, the employee said, "You know we have a tape recording of the kid saying he didn't want to come home . . . he wanted to stay."

Discovering the tape was dramatic and revealing of pertinent fact. Polk got it because he talked to enough people and listened. He used the same technique—finding informed sources and listening—to learn that police had found common fibers on many of the young blacks being killed in Atlanta. That evidence was central to the police case that led to the conviction of Wayne Williams.

Seymour Hersh, another Pulitzer Prize winner, says this of

preparation: "I never interviewed anyone without knowing a lot about them, not even a casual interview. Beyond clips and talking to other people [who know the person], I spend two or three hours preparing the right questions. No great feat, but it really pays off."

A young reporter might think that Hersh gets to set his own rules because he's a star. That might be true now, but it also is part of the reason he became a star. You can make a career of excuses or you can park the excuses and prepare. Few reporters get all the time they want. But solid reporting requires that you find the time to prepare.

Nor should preparation be confined to interviewing. Beat reporters should constantly read books and magazines related to their areas. But whether you are a beat reporter or on general assignment, take this advice to heart:

Prepare. Go to the library and check the *Reader's Guide to Periodical Literature*; check the newspaper's library; talk to the librarian; talk to reporters who might have dealt with the subject. If the subject of the interview is an expert, try to read about the topic and the person. Remember, the further back you can check, the better. Many newspaper libraries have an "active" file that goes back five years; ask for material predating the "active" file.

Other obvious questions: the date and place of birth; economic and social circumstances of parents; a résumé that includes education, military service, alternative service (Peace Corps, etc.), job history. If you get the data from others, check it with the subject of your story. Most will be willing to confirm or correct and will be impressed that you prepared.

During the interview, note physical characteristics (hands, eyes, posture, most dominant physical feature, clothing); pay attention to the pattern of speech, volume of voice, facial expressions, gestures and general demeanor.

Polk and Hersh say the drudgery is what makes journalism work. Bob Scheer of the *Los Angeles Times* regards the *Reader's*

Guide to Periodical Literature as an important resource in preparing for interviews. He also suggests more than one interview session.

Polk's approach focuses on empathizing and steering the interviewee without interruption. He knows that there is more to conducting a successful interview than having a long list of incisive questions. How you ask them and how you listen matter too.

"A good reporter is a damn good listener. He or she works at listening . . . at making the source aware that he or she is listening, with interest.

"Heck, I've been even known to work at little facial tricks—a nod, a raised eyebrow, a bewildered slow headshake combined with a frown . . . facial expressions that steer a source with encouragement, challenge, or confusion and doubt that require more details and explanation from the source—all without interrupting him or her, whom we want to keep on talking."

Polk says that often all that is needed is to make clear you want help. He reminds us that many of those we want information from are dedicated workaholics who willingly talk about their obsession. Go to the person, sit back and suggest, "Tell me about what's going on."

Just as writing can be developed, so can listening. Life is seldom the way it appears; there is more. The more you open yourself to hearing what is said, the better you perceive what is going on.

Personnel specialists trained to match applicants with jobs employ interviewing techniques that can be useful to journalists. They outline the things they want to cover during the interview. It is too easy to be diverted into an interesting subject. An outline can help you remember important questions.

Making a person comfortable enough to open up is often as much a function of time as of technique. Even the willing, articulate interviewee will add details when it is clear that there is no need to hurry. Being open and at ease during an interview is less of a problem when you know the source and the source knows and trusts you. But many times you have to build trust on the spot. Remember Polk's advice—be a good listener; be patient and show interest in what the *interviewee wants* to tell.

There are times when the interviewee insists on telling you things you might not regard as important. Be careful; the person might lead you to an important aspect you knew nothing about. You should have questions prepared but you also should be alert to encouraging the interviewee to talk about aspects unknown to you.

The comfort factor is especially important when you are dealing with a nervous person or someone who is not articulate or is possibly afraid of appearing foolish. One technique is to ask them what they can tell you that will help you understand.

Pleasant surprises during an interview most likely will not come if the time is short or the setting is filled with distractions. Show an interest in what the person wants to tell you and convey the sense that you are not in a hurry.

You need a place where distractions—particularly the telephone—are minimal. For that reason, the interviewee's office can be the worst place. The key is to find a place where concentration on the subject is encouraged. But whether or not the circumstances are conducive to relaxing, you still need the information.

Personnel interviewers are trained to dig for specific details. One device they use that a reporter could benefit from is asking the open-ended question or directive that is built around a superlative. Examples:

"Tell me about the *worst* beating you received."

"What is the *most* rewarding part of being governor?"

"Tell me the circumstances surrounding the *first* time you noticed money was missing?"

Preparation should reflect the importance of the interview. If an interview is worth doing, it is worth preparing for.

USING A TAPE RECORDER

On the use of a tape recorder during an interview, I have no great advice to offer. There are reporters who want no part of a tape recorder. They feel it gets in the way of people relaxing and talking freely.

Perhaps it is a matter of a self-fulfilling prophecy—if you feel uneasy about it, the feeling is transmitted to the interviewee. Obviously, taping can assist accuracy. But using a tape recorder can add to reporting and writing time because the temptation is to replay the entire interview. That is not a problem with written notes. You might try writing from notes and then checking important sections of the interview tape for details or quotes.

If you use a recorder, be certain it is portable and reliable, and that you know how it works. Set it up at the start of the interview as if it were routine.

Before leaving for the interview, test the batteries and make a voice-level test on the tape. Set the volume level correctly and once the interview starts, leave the recorder alone except to change tapes. The same is true with taping a telephone interview: Be prepared.

And just as a photographer should never be caught without enough film, a reporter should have enough recording tape and fresh batteries. Don't leave home without them.

You can shorten the time required to find key parts of an interview by using a recorder with a counter. Set it at zero when starting and mark the number on the tape where a remark can be found.

TAKING NOTES

Keep all notes, press releases and other information that you used in writing a story for at least twenty-four hours. Most newspapers will provide a standard reporter's notebook. On the cover is a place for your name, the subject and the date. Add your phone number and address in case you lose the notebook.

Also use the cover to index contents by material and dates—especially when you fill more than one notebook for a story or series. That makes it easier to check research if there are questions later. Be certain to use full identification of the interviewee—name, title, age, date, time and place of interview—and how you got to know the person who is not a regular source. If you are investigating something illegal, such details are even more important.

If you interview a hostile source, record what the person was wearing, the setting (furnishings, items on desk), who was present, and the day and hour. Some people might later deny that the interview took place; others might say it was idle talk over a beer.

Save your notes and file them systematically. Be meticulous in taking notes, and as soon as you return from the interview, expand your notes as fully as possible.

PROTECTING INNOCENTS

Bob Scheer is known for his *Playboy* interview with Jimmy Carter in which the presidential candidate confessed to having lust in his heart. Scheer formerly worked for *Ramparts* magazine, which cut a noticeable swath by digging out and publishing exclusive information about U.S. involvement in Vietnam. He holds several views not found in most journalism textbooks.

First, he regards studied neutrality as much the same as studied indifference. "You need a point of view; a position for reference . . . neutrality intrudes; neutrality can be deceptive."

Scheer offers this indelicate advice for writing: "When you have a good story to tell, relax, reach back and put some piss into it—something that reveals it is human and real."

His is a call to fill the space with evidence of humanity, of things that give meaning and insights rather than rhetoric and form. Lest you think he was advocating hot-rod Gonzo journalism, the ultimate expression of a reporter's ego, he added: "There is no room for advocacy." The reporter must never become a participant.

Scheer also advises reporters to protect sources who are not public figures, such as the female member of Jerry Falwell's church who on first contact criticized the Moral Majority preacher harshly. She knew Scheer was a newsman. Still, he told her to think about her words; they could very well be picked up by the wires and appear in her hometown paper. He says showing such concern for people pays and leads to getting even better information.

A note of caution about interviews presented in a question-and-answer format: Too many are just plain dull. Of course, as a subcategory of newspaper writing, nothing can match the reporting of government for dull and drab. At its worst, government reporting can be dry enough to curl wallpaper. Such reporting focuses on committee actions and never introduces the human element.

Which brings us to another tip for those who cover government: *When reporting politicians and bureaucrats, remember that institutions do not make decisions—people make decisions.*

Through interviews, a reporter can learn what values were taken into account and how the decision was made. Not many years ago it was thought of as the story behind the story. But there is no need to invent categories. Just find the people involved and interview them.

INTERVIEWING VERSUS POLLING

From time to time, newspapers conduct polls. There are polls that are trustworthy, but precious few newspapers will stand the expense required to avoid the pitfalls common in sampling.

A bigger problem newspapers have with polls is drawing too many conclusions from the facts gathered.

The better polls involve detailed and sophisticated interviewing methods and discover important nuances throughout a range of responses. They seldom suggest the discovery of one common set of mind among many. Polls of such detail and nuance reflect reality.

Most editors, however, want polls that predict election results. Which is where many newspaper polls go wrong. Polls present a picture of what existed for a brief period. Though attitudes and preferences can and frequently do change, too often newspapers report the poll results as if they were absolute and unchanging. Reporters should be very, very wary in stating what polls reveal. It is easy to overdraw the bank of information.

Man-on-the-street interviews, the hackneyed quick-hit, one-question jobs, are not good measures of what individuals think or feel. For one thing, some people anticipate what they are expected to say; others will try to respond in acceptable ways. An interview provides a chance to probe feelings and pursue reasoning. Understanding, whether by interview or by poll, takes time.

INVESTIGATIVE REPORTING

The cliché has it that every reporter should be an investigative reporter. True, but not every story is worth digging into deeply. Good investigative editors and reporters have two traits that might appear contradictory: They check out good tips, and they know when to halt and when to press on. News judgment is central to good use of time. It also helps to be able to sense when you are headed down blind alleys. *Time, lots of time, can be wasted stumping around with an eye stuck to a spyglass.*

To avoid wasting time, move an investigation along in stages.

Qualify it before you dive in headfirst. And you might as well face it: Most investigations that are published are based on information that is received early on. You generally have to flesh out the details, but for the most part, you have the essence of what you need when you start.

There are exceptions: Donald Bartlett and James Steele's work for the *Philadelphia Inquirer* dug into records to discover the inequity of federal income tax rules and regulations. More famous was the Watergate investigation by Robert Woodward and Carl Bernstein, which entailed digging out things done covertly. One involved giving coherence to readily available materials; the other required a different sense of discovery, starting with Woodward's curiosity about expensively dressed lawyers representing burglars.

If visions of Pulitzers dance in your head, keep in mind that investigations present the toughest of journalistic challenges. Lots of people know lots of things they can't prove. A journalist needs solid evidence.

Information is not enough; you must gather information you can publish. Too many investigative reporters know things they can't publish because they cannot get it on the record. Newspapers should have standards, and among the more important should be attribution to establish credibility. If your editors will let you attribute information to anonymous sources, life becomes easier. It is, however, often unfair to the accused.

Getting into print should not be the dominant consideration during an investigation. Fairness and fullness should be kept central. Be extremely reluctant to go into print without being able to share with the reader where the information came from. A newspaper has nothing if it lacks credibility.

You do well to write your revelations in plain, unsupercharged language. Shun "informed sources." Name the accusers. The need to identify sources means that you have to approach them differently. Any reporter can find "sources" who will discredit others—if the discrediting can be done anonymously.

The arguments for publishing accusations made anonymously will not be presented here. Doing so might endorse them. Journalists have a sacred obligation to level with the readers. Pass by the "good" story unless you can reveal the source. It is shabby to nail public figures and try to justify the story on grounds that they are fair game and must be kept honest. That is hit-and-run journalism, not thorough, not balanced.

Such attacks also help decide who will seek public office. Prospective candidates who are intelligent and able can't help being put off by the "let's get the dirty bastards" brand of reporting. Cleveland's municipal finances became national news when the city faced default of debts. Such mismanagement can be traced to the quality of public officials holding power, and that can be greatly influenced by a blood-lusting style of reporting. Good people *can* be discouraged from seeking public office. In Cleveland they were.

The ideal for investigative reporting is an open mind not easily convinced by explanations that lack completeness and concrete evidence. Avoid either extreme; don't let people easily explain away a problem and don't decide too soon that someone is "guilty." A source will know when you have blood in your eye, and likely will hesitate to respond openly and fully to questions.

The problem can begin with the research. Journalists, like anyone else, tend to accept the printed word. If an earlier reporter portrayed a person as a boob or a perfect clown, reading the stories could color your inquiry. And your approach would, in turn, color that person's response. Bias can be subtle. Nurture the open mind.

And be reluctant to focus a report on motives. Asking *why* something was done might help you understand what happened. But as a journalist you should emphasize *what* was done. Provide context for the actions, but be chary of trying to plumb motives, and do not try to characterize motivations. Why someone did something will always be open to argument. Be content to report what was done and in what context.

During an investigation, you should set out to understand what happened. Set aside your judgments until you have completed your work. Challenge explanations that paint some people as good and others as bad. Those judgments might prove true, but concentrate on checking facts rather than seeking facts that support your first impression.

When reporting on legal agreements, read the documents rather than accept what someone says. Be certain the contract wasn't altered by a later agreement or a side agreement.

One common newspaper investigation involves purchases of expensive equipment, such as computers, by governments. Losing bidders often become willing tipsters. The losers commonly complain that the low bid was not taken or units were purchased that cannot perform as well as those shunned.

Start investigations of public purchases by understanding the criteria the buyers used. Public contracts normally require specifications. The first question should be: "Did the winner meet the specifications?" If several bids met specifications, ask the buyers what other considerations were weighed before the choice was made. And there is the common tactic of rigging specifications to favor a bidder.

To investigate awards of contracts, you must understand the process that was followed and find out whether the laws and regulations for such bidding were followed. And after you have understood all that good stuff, remember to ask: "So what?" Is the public affected? Did the public pay more than it should have? Was comparable equipment available for less money?

Find the paper documents—the criteria, the specifications, the written justifications. Go to the people who will be the users of the equipment. Ask them what they need and how it compares to what they got. Were they consulted?

The public interest requires that a useful service or product was acquired at a competitive, reasonable price.

All this sounds pretty mundane and it is. Anyone writing a screenplay about a hot-rock investigative reporter would be tempted to include a scene in which the bad person is confronted. Many investigations do produce someone who is clearly culpable. But the wise investigative reporter will park the Sam Spade tough-boy routine and leave it parked.

To begin with, an investigation is in a lot of trouble if you enter the confrontive interview needing information or evidence from the accused. If you are in that position when the confrontive interview is set, your investigation is shaky. Confession or even acknowledgment of responsibility is likely only when you can show the accused that you have gathered material that points directly at the person.

The point is that first you should work around anyone you suspect might be culpable. Before you interview that person, you should have as many answers as possible. The accused is unlikely to fill any gaps in your knowledge.

All that hints at method. If you want to know more about techniques and tap into a valuable resource, join Investigative Reporters and Editors, Inc., a nonprofit organization based at the University of Missouri journalism school in Columbia. It is a gold mine.

But attitude can be more important than method. Without an open mind, you jeopardize fairness and balance. The reporter should not be a prosecutor.

If you enter an interview with blood in your eye, stop. Go take a cold shower. Remember that how you ask a question can affect the answer. If you have someone dead to rights, let that come out in the facts you reveal, not in the manner by which you reveal them.

Interviews should be planned. Hold your hard questions, the questions most likely to cause the interviewee to end the interview, until you have asked the less upsetting questions. As for style and tone in an interview, the shorter question is best.

Asking good questions requires thought, and the fewer the questions you need to ask, the better. Too many reporters forget you can move an elbow with a feather as well as with a hammer. The feather leaves no bruises and requires less labor. Don't try to overcome lack of preparation with a brusque approach.

There will be times when to dig out information you must be aggressive and challenging. But your job remains to get it full and fair or forget it.

3

WRITING

Let's get one thing straight: All this stuff about writing being hard work is just that—stuff. Writing is not hard work. Bucking hay bales, shocking feed, carrying hod, digging ditches and unloading a boxcar filled with cement bags are hard work. Fun is being paid to do something you want to do. And reporting and writing is that something, isn't it?

Some people argue that writers are born, not made. That is propaganda designed to restrict the membership list at The Writers Club. Writing might be easier for some than for others, but clear writing can be learned. Pure writing is a craft that is born in the ear and the eye. No one is born knowing how. Read a lot, find a good editor and keep plugging away. Be willing to rewrite your copy—hone sentences, smooth paragraphs, emphasize clarity.

Reporters with serious writing problems have helped themselves by shifting the emphasis from writing to storytelling. While writing seems to emphasize form, storytelling emphasizes substance. If you *truly* understand the subject and if it has news value, you should be able to write a story that others will want to read.

Experience is important. It is easier now to convert my notes into news stories than it was immediately after college. Gathering the information was relatively easy, but the blank page waiting in the typewriter dampened my shirt and hurt my head. The fear of failure can do that to you.

Oh, I knew the issues that first year. I knew the issues and I knew how each of the commissioners voted. I even had some quotes. All that was in my notebook, and I had even checked how to spell the names. Still I sat sweating. Neither Strunk nor White could help me, though I had read and reread *The Elements of Style*. Each of my sentences and paragraphs was forced through my brain under great pressure from my soul.

That pain still strikes occasionally, but it has eased. The key for me was to realize that every writer must be a storyteller, and to tell a story, you must understand it.

Your job as reporter is first to understand—take your story apart and squeeze it until you know what is there; drag it close to your nose for a sniff. When you are familiar with the parts, then go to a private corner and put it into a coherent whole. If you are confused or unclear, the reader hasn't much chance to learn from your writing.

I use the word "understand" to mean something different from the word "know." During my first weeks on the job, I knew the votes and the issues on the City Commission of Ottawa, Kansas, in 1963; what I lacked was understanding of what they meant to the readers.

I have seldom edited a writer who understood an event who had serious trouble choosing the correct elements for a lead. Nor will a reporter who understands the context of what he or she is reporting have a serious problem in organizing the information. If you command your material, you can apply the principles of good writing.

That might not be true for every novelist, essayist or short-story writer. But it is for the journalist, whose job is to know and tell. In telling, you should present useful information in a way that is easy to follow and, when possible, compelling.

That involves both reporting and writing.

For many years I would have said that good writing is always simple and clear. I no longer think that newswriting must be simple to be good. It must, however, be clear.

And keep in mind that not every story is worth more than checking the facts, stacking them in the inverted pyramid and moving on. (It is interesting, though, how two reporters can treat the same subject with remarkably different results. A curious person who applies imagination will always hold an advantage.)

When you start writing, remember the scope of the assignment. If you get a press release and are told, "Check this out and write me a short," you know what is wanted. Select the basic nut of information and write an unadorned, straightforward news item. Check the details, write them plainly and simply and then hit the send button. (Pardon the computer talk.)

Not every story requires deep thinking or prolonged inquiry. Some things are so clear and ripe that they need only to be picked and put into the paper. This is exemplified by a revelation of startling information—such as a surprise resignation. Such a story is rare enough, but when it comes, pull out the inverted pyramid and pump away.

But always heed the direction to "check this out." Do not assume that a story in another paper is accurate, full or fair; the same goes for electronic reports. And always check out news releases—if for no other reason than that typists often make errors. Occasionally in checking you will find a better story. As soon as you are certain, tell your editor that the scope of the story has changed.

For stories that go beyond the bare-bone essentials, you need to talk with your editor-supervisor. Talk before you start the serious reporting. Before you start writing, get the message on how far to go.

The scope of the story will help fix the length. Ask when you must turn it in. The time you have for writing determines a number of things. For instance, when David Broder sat down to write the story of John Hinckley Jr.'s shooting of President Reagan, he was faced with time pressure. Working for a wire service can teach you what Broder used for his story—the straightforward inverted pyramid. You can also learn to use that format by reading the wire service reports. No one is a journeyman until he or she can write such stories almost instinctively.

You can and should learn to write at a pace associated with deadlines. Too many people struggle unnecessarily. Study your material, understand it, and then write it.

HARD NEWS OR FEATURES

Some folks divide journalism into hard news and features. Hard news is written plainly; features can offer side trips down country lanes with time to stop and describe the wrinkles of those who live there. Hard news is generally thought of as having perishable value; to delay it is to lessen or kill its interest. Features are less connected to the when.

But it is needlessly limiting to view stories as being either features or hard news. Many newspapers, large and small, are learning that blurring the distinctions between features and hard news can benefit the readers. This is done by putting more news in features and more human elements in hard news.

It is important to remember that you should be writing for the reader. Don't permit the telling to overwhelm the story. The best newswriting works so smoothly that it comes very close to being invisible.

That advice rules out prideful presentations of needless details before getting to the point. An example of what to avoid: "Smoke curled from his pipe and wafted upward to the green-painted ceiling of his office. His feet, shod in scuffed Florsheims, were propped on the corner of his desk. He eyed his visitor as he mulled the questions put to him."

Newspaper reporters should be reluctant to convey a sense of place without tying it closely to some action. Revealing details should reveal something that will enhance understanding. Revealing details should be made to perform essential work. If the place isn't central to the reporting, forget it. Writing adorned with minutiae does not help the reader understand.

The more flexible approach to newswriting permits you to deal with subjects of importance while maintaining a special concern for answering the questions "So what?" and "Whom does it affect?"

The answers to those two questions should be central to the writing. The inverted pyramid dictates an emphasis on the most dramatic elements of the story, but even that format does not guarantee the reader will understand the consequences of what you are reporting. If you gather information with those two questions in mind, it will greatly shape the writing.

The *Minneapolis Tribune* used that approach in reporting publicly financed pensions. Members of the city council approved generous pension benefits but failed to raise taxes enough to pay the cost. When the pensions were due, the money to pay them would not be there. (Note "members of the city council" and not "the city council"; persons, not institutions, do things. Think of government that way. Report it that way. Write it that way.)

The first stories were straightforward and focused on the unfunded liabilities. Those were unadorned, hard-news stories.

But the writing of subsequent stories was largely dictated by the reporting approach, which emphasized understanding who was affected and how. We set out to tell how the city came to such a pass, and to tell it in ways that made it easy for the reader to understand the why and how. This required finding the persons who made the pension decisions and asking them why. The prize-winning series also reported what the money meant in the lives of those reliant on pensions, and the disparity of bigger pensions awarded for fewer years of service. We also showed how the plan wouldn't work financially.

The tone of the writing was set as the reporters kept in mind the purpose of each article. The purpose dictated the reporting approach, and in turn, the writing style.

Both style and approach need to be appropriate. The tone that's right for the bright, short feature is not suitable for describing a funeral.

And be sure that the persons chosen as illustrations are typical. If they are not, using them as examples distorts reality.

THE LEAD

I'm uncertain where I got the definition, but I can tell you one thing all good leads have in common: *They are clear and easy to read and could not be used accurately on any other story.* That means the lead should focus on the elements unique to the story. Lest you think this puts you in a cage of small dimensions, relax.

Suppose you are reporting a meeting of the state pollution control board. The subject begs for a boring telling; certainly, few board meetings offer bright opportunities. Witness:

"The state pollution control board Thursday considered a list of alternatives and took under advisement staff recommendations of what to do about the discharge of untreated sewage into the Muddy River by polluters in the area."

Such a lead shows what can happen when the reporter does not take hold of the subject and get serious about assessing it. The reporter let the story write itself, which is O.K. if the event is interesting. Actions of government agencies, however, seldom are.

The remedy is to be a storyteller, a person who distills and assesses and *then* lays it before the readers.

Among the unaccomplished, that could be a license for all sorts of journalistic crimes, ranging from hyping a lead to substituting opinion for fact. (Remember to make distinctions among fact, opinion and judgment.)

This advice assumes intelligence, professional detachment, a sense of balance and fair play, a knowledge and love of words—and some basic education in journalism. And never forget the need to be full and fair.

Let's return to the account of the pollution board meeting. If the example indeed told the most interesting, compelling thing that happened at the meeting, it represented a nonstory.

When that happens, tell your editor. Don't say, "There's nothing there." That's a judgment. Instead, give the editor a rundown of the things that led you to think there was no story.

To provide useful, compelling information in a story on pollution, you have to flee the board meeting. The meeting might be useful for background, but the story can be told better from elsewhere. Consider, let us say, that Riverwhack Industries is pumping hydrogen sulfide into the air and wood pulp residue into the water, creating a stink and smothering aquatic life.

Start by learning what Riverwhack produces and by what process. Perhaps Riverwhack makes the newsprint your story will be published on.

Make clear the connections between what is good (making newsprint) and what is bad (polluting). No industry is in the business of making pollution. Tell how loggers rely on the mill to provide them a market. Report the economic chain from forest to consumer (and perhaps even to landfill). Give the reader an understanding of those who make a living from the polluting activity and what it would cost to stop the pollution.

A fullness of reporting is fundamental to a fullness of writing. You cannot write accurately and interestingly about things you do not understand.

Two tests for every lead: Is it too wordy? Do you support the lead elsewhere in the story? And don't use questions for leads. (Well, O.K., once in a while, but make it rare.)

CLICHÉS

The clearest evidence of inadequate reporting is clichéd, hyped writing: "A lone gunman stalked . . ." "During a high-speed chase . . ."

Those phrases appear in story after story, and they fail because they make all the stories sound much the same. Better to concentrate on particulars—details of what happened. Instead of writing "high-speed chase," talk to the officer so you can report the precise speed at which the cars were traveling, and add such details as whether the road was crowded and whether there were any close calls with other people or vehicles.

Try to determine why the driver was speeding in the first place. Did he have a record for unsafe driving?

Readers want details—not warmed-over clichés.

When you understand what happened, there is less chance that you will overreach for verbs that cut and dance, jump and swim, and all other sorts of cute things. The facts, presented in a coherent context, will be enough—if you understand what happened. Concentrate on what is unique, and clichés will be less of a problem.

CHRONOLOGY

Once you're sold on the importance of understanding, of *truly* knowing, you come to another journalistic hurdle—the clear telling of complicated information. As noted earlier, you make the task easier if you find an example that illustrates how the story affects people.

But when you become stuck in telling something, heed the wisdom of Lewis Carroll: Start at the beginning and tell the story chronologically.

That opens the door to numerous storytelling formats, including use of the narrative. The style isn't fancy, but few things make more compelling reading than the words of a witness or participant. Sometimes all a reporter has to do is ask, "What happened?" and stick the response into the paper.

Getting as quickly as you can to a chronological telling often means the reader has a better chance of understanding the event.

Whatever method you choose, keep it clear.

VARIETY IN WRITING

Newspapers need to present stories in a variety of ways. But whatever approach you use, be eager to tell readers why the story is important. Yield that nut of information by at least the fourth paragraph. Give them the answer to "So what?" Tell them why they should care by telling them whom it affects and how.

Using forms other than the inverted pyramid requires a degree of patience in telling (and reading) the story. The essence of the inverted pyramid is that it distills the important stuff up high. If you shun the inverted pyramid, remember that readers do not share the writer's advantage:

The writer knows what the story is about. The readers must learn that from the story. Tell them sooner rather than later—not in the lead every time, but don't wait long.

Some writers complain that "the flow" is ruined by the requirement to tell why early. Tough. The newspaper should serve readers, not writers.

And of course the desire to write brightly does not permit a newspaper journalist to mix fact, opinion and judgment into news reporting. Remember the differences as illustrated here:

Fact: The train is running late.

Opinion: We will be late arriving at the station.

Judgment: This train is never on time!

RHYTHM AND PACE, TEXTURE AND TONE

Although good newspaper writing should always be clear, there is more to good writing than clarity. Reading is a treat when the rhythm is right—stop, go, pause, start, feel, smell. Wonders can be done by a writer with a feel for the right word, a writer with an ear that picks up the way people speak.

A good reporter-writer provides a sense of place born of knowing that different speakers use the language differently. Take your ears to a workingman's bar after hearing a university professor lecture. Each form of expression can have its own texture and tone. *Adopt the pace, tone and texture and the idioms of the people you are writing about—keep all of it true to the place and the people.*

Pace dictates rhythm and it can help set tone. We can produce prose with the characteristics of poetry if the words are made to work together. There can even be clear hints of cadence—an imperative pace that readers can follow if they want to understand the life and the people at the place you describe.

To do these things you must take hold of the story and shape it for the ease and pleasure of the reader. Give it a beginning, a middle and an end. Shape it. Start by knowing the focus. Exercise judgment as to what is more important.

But never forget that your job as a newspaper reporter-writer is to provide useful information. We inform, entertain or influence—or a combination of the three. To succeed we must be understood.

TRYING TOO HARD

One common problem for writers who have the courage to stretch is that they can't resist our old enticing friend, the over-reach.

Want protection? Resist the urge to invent words. Shun the temptation to build a supercharged sentence. Do not have an inanimate object, such as an airplane, doing something animate: "Its wheels anticipating the touch of the tarmac . . ." The turn of the phrase is beautiful, but it is trickery.

And just to prove that rules are not always right, here is a lead that violates several, yet is one to admire:

"The monster that eats cars and spits them out in fist-size steel cuds is in operation here, chewing and digesting a one-ton car in 45 seconds while separating the main course from the garbage."

There is a lead that informs, is easy to read yet provides a vivid image.

A good journalist keeps the lead in mind and buttresses it. The writer who gave us the "fist-size steel cuds" metaphor needs to explain what is the main course and what constitutes the garbage. Nor should he forget to tell how the machine was developed, why, and what it means to the readers and the readers' economy.

We hear often that good writers rely on verbs to do their heavy work and shun adjectives as being sugar-coated rotters. It can't be denied—selecting the correct verb gives precision to the writing and reduces the number of words needed.

And stir around in your box of nouns and pronouns; picking the right one of those can do wonders as well. The right combination of nouns and verbs can reduce the need for adjectives and adverbs.

But there is a danger in drawing too much attention to the mechanics of writing. The beginner is better served by remembering first to understand and then to write. As I've said before, think of writing as the act of expressing what you understand.

Your choice of words should always remain connected to what you are reporting. Make the words appropriate to the person, and to the event, that you are reporting. Never treat writing as a separate exercise in wordsmanship.

I recall reading in a West Coast paper about two high school students who were charged with stuffing their newborn infant into a sack and leaving it by the road. That is one hell of a story and it does not require a wordsman to provide drama. Yet the writer went wrong, first in selecting the lead, which was about a high school girl wearing a jacket to hide her pregnancy. A teen trying to hide her pregnancy is compelling, but how many times have two kids stuffed their newborn child into a grocery bag and dumped it by the road? That element was hidden deep in the story. It is not sufficient excuse to point out that this fact had been reported in earlier editions.

Then, not content to let the story tell itself, the writer turned the sentences into a playbox for words and from there went dabbling into unwarranted assumptions: "In San Francisco, people aren't stunned by anything."

That is untrue. Being stunned in San Francisco helps keep the shrinks there driving late-model Porsches. The statement tells more about the writer than it does about the sensibilities of San Franciscans.

Characterizing events rather than presenting specifics is where the writer went astray. Let the facts do the work. Don't tell me. Show me. Take the writer out of the story and let others provide the assessments. Allow the event to be itself; don't impose on it.

Another reporter fell overboard while writing about a man not known to have uttered a word for seven years. Again, the trouble came in reaching for sharp characterizations rather than just laying out the story.

The lead told us that the man smiled with his eyes. Nonsense. We smile with our mouths. Cover every part of a person's face except the eyes and you can't tell what the person is doing unless it involves tears or redness. You smile with your mouth (unless you are Irish).

The reporter also wrote that the man "smiles quietly." He should try smiling noisily. "Smiles quietly" is a cliché.

These mistakes resulted from not thinking about the meaning of words. Words have roots and origins.

Permit me to rant further:

Do not be quick to create new "wise" words (healthwise, moneywise). Otherwise, you could get crosswise with the reader.

Do not convert verbs to nouns, or nouns to verbs, as in "Despite its excesses, the book is a worthwhile read." We have enough verbs and enough nouns to do our work. We need not invent new ones. (Are you listening, ye wizards at *Time* magazine?)

And if your purpose in writing is to be understood, remember that the longer the sentence, the more difficult it is to comprehend. As with bridges, longer sentences require more careful construction.

Another common failing among writers who want to dazzle is that they dress a story in atmospherics. "A light drizzle was graying the cold, concrete canyons of the Big Apple when it happened." That lead could be used on any report of something that happened on any rainy day in New York City. Unique to the story it is not; nor does it reveal useful or compelling information.

When in doubt, count the adjectives. Most adjectives can be used in many, many places. *Search for the nouns and verbs that define the story.* If you do that before you start to write, the lead should be easier to write.

The story about the drizzle that was graying the canyons of Manhattan also gave us "the taxi-blasted canyons of Manhattan." Use atmospherics and adjectives like paprika—for color—and be certain not to use too much.

Years of reading newspapers have convinced me that the sports page is the common nesting place for the nonsense called elegant variation. Consider this excess: "In all, five national high school records, 12 California State Meet bests and four San Diego County standards tumbled." Records . . . bests . . . standards—ugh!

Many teachers send the writer in search of the striking, revealing quote. Its value is obvious. But all quotes are not created equal; you would do well to be choosy.

A common mistake is overusing the partial quote—one, two, three or four words stuck in the middle of a sentence. Short, partial quotes are graphic roadblocks that flare from the page to halt the eye. Save quotes for their main purpose—sharing with the reader words that have a quality that elevates them or otherwise makes them worthy of being transmitted precisely.

Don't use partial quotes when attribution is clear without them or when there is nothing memorable about the phrasing. In story after story, sentence after sentence, you can clutter copy with partial quotes. Don't.

JOURNALESE

Charles McDowell, a Washington correspondent for the *Richmond Times-Dispatch*, laments that newspaper writing has a language the public does not share.

The classic, stylized conventions of wire service writing are with us still. At its worst, the most serious question considered is whether to place the day before or after the verb in lead sentences.

We also add to the artificiality of newspaper writing by our needless habit of attributing everything. Most attribution makes sense, but often the "he said"/"she said" does little more than slow the reading.

Another symptom of journalese: quotes that are formal and stilted rather than reflective of the way people speak. We are reluctant to use "ain't" and we seldom include an incomplete sentence even though people speak that way. Don't throw in an incomplete sentence for the hell of it, but then don't use quotes that way either.

McDowell says that too often American journalism uses language that is surging, gasping, lurching—essentially artificial.

He tells of an editor who gained a reputation for rapidly improving the writing at several newspapers. He simply insisted that long, complicated sentences be shortened, beginning with the startling suggestion that there be one idea to a sentence.

Writing for newspapers imposes tests of accuracy, completeness, fairness and balance. Those tests must be applied if substance is to hold its rightful place over form. But if we are to do the best we can, we must stop writing in tongues. Journalese, in all its manifestations, should be shunned.

As for style, write as if you were preparing a letter to an intelligent friend. That includes both vocabulary and tone. Learn the marvels of understatement and remember to hug your copy of Strunk and White's *The Elements of Style.* Keep a dictionary within reach when writing, and use it.

Most newspapers could be made more readable by rewriting. Be willing to rewrite, to try suggestions. Rewriting is best done by the author. Although there are exceptions, at most papers too little time is given to serious editing. It should be of equal importance to the writing. Keep in mind that if you always press the deadline and never provide ample time for editing, you can't benefit from editing. Many reporters hold copy until the deadline nears to avoid editing. I recommend it for anyone whose copy is perfect.

4
SOURCES

The essence of reporting is finding what you need to help the reader understand. You cannot understand something until you get it and that almost always means you need sources.

The beat reporter's sources are obvious. The courts reporter, for instance, needs access to judges, their clerks and their bailiffs, and he needs a list of home telephone numbers as well as office numbers.

Acquiring phone numbers can be as simple as asking for a copy of a county directory or a courts directory. Or asking the person who covered the beat ahead of you for his or her list of phone numbers. If there are more than a handful of people in an agency, a bureau or a court, there will be a directory. However, it may not include home numbers. You can get many of those numbers by checking local telephone directories. If you are blessed with a library that keeps old directories, you can get numbers for persons who have stopped listing their telephones. Crisscross directories from previous years can help; they are indexed by street address and telephone number as well as by name.

It's common courtesy as well as foresighted to ask key persons, such as clerks and bailiffs, whether they would be willing to talk from their homes in an emergency. But when starting a beat, wait awhile before asking for this information. If people are not listed in the directories, it is by their choice. It is doubtful they will give telephone numbers to a stranger.

In covering the courts, cultivate the judges. Court staff people can help too. But remember, no one can be compelled to give you a home number.

When assigned to a new beat, write names in a notebook and check the spellings with each person you meet. Ask the friendly ones on the beat to help identify others and explain how things work.

Important as the persons with titles are, you need to cultivate informal sources. They are everywhere. Secretaries, law clerks, computer operators, janitors—all know portions of what goes on. But, just as you know better than to swallow the official line, you listen to the janitor with a skeptical ear. Check out what every source tells you and ask yourself, "How does that person know that?"

Some reporters find it easy to talk with almost everyone. They walk into data processing rooms as if they belonged there and strike up conversations. It is a skill worth cultivating. When you want to interview welfare recipients, go to the welfare office itself rather than ask a caseworker to find a welfare recipient for you. That prevents being set up with a case that is not representative.

Let's say you need to find parents and teenagers for a story on how they solve the problem of allowing increased freedom while still providing protection and guidance. Call on some ministers. Their work as counselors makes them good sources.

To get stories before others do, and to get stories that others do not get, a beat reporter absolutely, positively must work the sources—every day, every week. *When a week has passed during which an important source has not been contacted, on the next day call that source.* Talk football or the weather or any other subjects of interest, but always conduct some business as well. The purpose of your call is to learn something that can be put into the newspaper—for the readers. But remember to come across as a person gathering news rather than a machine harvesting information. A common mistake is to use the approach typified by the question: "You don't have anything for me, do you?" Take time to talk with sources and do not act as if you are imposing on them. Your work is important. Convey that sense.

When covering government, sometimes you should go to the very top. A clerk refuses to provide public documents, and the director of the department won't help? Go to the mayor, the governor, the attorney general—if all else fails, think big.

FRIENDLY, BUT NEVER FRIENDS

Be mindful that most editors once upon a time were reporters, and some find it hard to drop that role. The worst editors for beginning reporters to work under have enduring friendships with their old news sources. If you have such an editor, pray that he or she will listen to an old source, take notes to pass on to you and then tell the source to deal with you—the reporter handling the story.

Pray also that your editor doesn't expect you never to be beaten on a story. If he does, you are much more at the mercy of your news sources than good newspapers should allow.

Mark this down: *Be friendly with sources but never, not ever, become friends.* Friendships with sources will get in the way. Remember, you exist professionally for two purposes:

1. To know, comprehend, understand.
2. To tell.

Some reporters make friends with sources to avoid being beaten. This is unprofessional and creates a debt. The nature of friendship is that you give as well as receive. The only people a reporter should "give" to are editors and readers. *Your alle-*

giance to the reader leaves no room for returning "favors" to news sources.

Reporters who make friends with news sources are likely to find themselves operating under another disadvantage—they know things they cannot put into the paper unless they use unnamed sources. When you are convinced a source has a great story to tell, it is tempting to offer anonymity and perhaps even payment. Don't. Remember your debt to the reader. That debt includes revealing the sources of information.

And please, don't tell me about Watergate and "Deep Throat." That approach to reporting won the *Washington Post* two Pulitzers, one of which had to be returned.

Use sources to get things on the record. Let us say that the chief of police tips you that the mayor is a business partner with several shady characters in town—people with criminal records. Chances are the chief does not want it known that he spread the word. No problem. Go to the secretary of state's office and find out who incorporated the company; then you can cite the records rather than the person in a sensitive position.

RISKS

You need to recognize that there are dangers to reporters that are not figurative. On June 2, 1976, Don Bolles, an investigative reporter for the *Arizona Republic*, got into his car in a downtown Phoenix parking lot. The car exploded seconds later. As he lay mortally wounded, Bolles yelled the name of the man he believed responsible.

The First Amendment is powerful, but it does not provide armor plating. In cases where you are investigating possible criminals, it is vital that you have editors who recognize the dangers you might face.

Seymour Hersh, the reporter who broke the story of the

massacre of civilians at the village of My Lai in Vietnam, tells this story of his early reporting days in Chicago's City News Bureau.

Hearing that police had shot and killed a suspect, Hersh said:

"I go down to the [police] garage to be the first to talk to them. They get out and start talking to some of their buddies, telling them what they did. 'Yeah, we really got that nigger . . . we told him to run and we plugged him right in the back.' Okay, I had this. I'm 22, 23, it's about 1960, I've been on the job three or four months."

Hersh checked the autopsy report and found "he'd been shot so many times, but mostly in the back."

"I did nothing about it. I was scared to death."

Why did a reporter with the convictions and courage of Seymour Hersh do nothing about what he heard? It went back to an experience he had had with an editor at the City News Bureau.

In that instance, Hersh hustled to the scene of a multiple killing and found that a man had gone wild, killing his wife, seven children and then himself. Hersh was dictating the details over the phone when the editor broke in on the line:

"My dear energetic Hersh—do, alas, the poor unfortunate victims happen to be of the American Negro persuasion?"

Hersh said yes.

"Cheap it out" the editor instructed—meaning one paragraph of two sentences.

That was Chicago in 1960.

Hersh's experiences illustrate how dependent a reporter is on the editor and publisher. He had no document to support what he said the officers said, no tape recording. It was a confession/accusation of cold-blooded murder that would have come down to the reporter's word against that of the police. Hersh had no doubts about what would have happened; his editors were not given to challenging police on behalf of blacks. Now he says, "It wouldn't happen today." Maybe. But in the 1970s I had a fellow editor who was angry that our newspaper's version of a shootout involving the death of a cop conflicted with the police version. He wanted to know what we were doing calling police liars. The account came from an eye-witness.

War stories aside, physical peril can be part of reporting. Don't operate as a lone hunter. Protect yourself professionally and personally by informing your editor of what you are finding. It should be made plain to potentially dangerous people whom you are investigating that others know what you know and that notes and documents are duplicated and locked safely away. Don Bolles recorded whom he was going to meet with. The information led to criminal charges.

By common experience, the killing of Don Bolles might seem melodramatic. But keep in mind that there are people who have no regard for the lives of others and who would gladly kill to protect themselves.

YOUR RIGHTS TO ACCESS

What do you do when you are stonewalled by a news source?

If you are covering the courts or the police, study your state's records laws so that you *understand* what you are enti-tled to have access to and when. Do not act helpless when your access to records is challenged. When you run into barriers, learn the proper response. Reciting the law to a balky bureau-crat can dissolve resistance. Carry in your billfold a card that lists the appropriate statute by number.

And for the convenience of the moment, make no agree-ments that suggest the public official is granting access as a favor. If it is a favor and not a legal right, it can be withdrawn on a whim.

You can't always get the information you need, in the form you need, when you need it. State law might give you right of access, but if the clerk with the key to the file cabinet refuses to unlock it, the law, for that particular moment, has no practical meaning.

The answer, in extreme cases, lies in having the newspaper's lawyer petition a judge to order compliance with the law. If your access is blocked, tell your supervising editor and ask for suggestions.

But there are many ways to get information. Anything in a file cabinet was put there by someone, and not always by the person blocking the way. Someone typed the material, someone else wrote the original report. Try to think of other sources. No government form started life in a file cabinet; think of others who know what you need to know. Be inventive. But do not take things. Theft is theft, no matter how good your intentions.

Today's better metropolitan newspapers are far beyond the breathless police reporting of the 1920s, when one reporter stood at the door asking questions while a colleague entered from the back to steal photos from the family dresser.

Consider the reporter who needed to talk with the family of a young child killed when a garage door at an apartment complex crushed him. The only things known were the name and age of the child, his address, the cause of death (crushed larynx). The phone at the child's address was not answered.

The reporter went to the scene and knocked on doors. Some reporters are reluctant to do that; they consider it unfeeling and a bit ghoulish.

Relax. Most people touched by tragedy are eager to try to explain what happened. Take the time to ask for exact spellings of names and to verify information. Don't ask another reporter who isn't certain and then go with a consensus guess. Look it up. Check for yourself. If you want to upset survivors, spell a name wrong or get the facts askew. Don't let your uneasiness cause you to rush or skip over details. Where death is involved, remember that funeral directors routinely gather much of the information you need.

Why bother? Doesn't it smack of sensationalism?

That depends on how fully the story is reported and from what perspective it is pursued. If the story has no purpose other than to reveal the grisliest details of an injury, then the argument for not doing it has grounds.

But too many young reporters (some older ones too) find it beneath them to deal with death and grief. They act as if reporting simple, human stories somehow makes the reporter less professional. The more extreme among them are reluctant to report stories that involve talking with ordinary, unelected, everyday citizens thrust into the news by tragedy.

In the death of the youngster caught by the garage door, a good reporter would ask such questions as: How does the garage door operate? Is there a reversing mechanism that stops the door when it meets resistance before it is completely closed? Are the garage entrances at the complex near play areas used by children? Was the child playing a game, racing to get under the door before it closed? Or did the child slip from the top of an incline and fall? Have other residents seen children playing near the door? And what about building codes? Is it legal to have doors without reversing mechanisms? Did the door have one that didn't work? Was the mechanism disconnected? Is the same danger still present?

These are questions that occur to survivors, to readers who have children, to apartment managers, to safety inspectors, to insurance companies—persons who might, if they get enough information, do something to prevent the death of other children.

That is public service. Such reporting is useful and legitimate, even if some people become angry when inquiries are made. The value of the story does not hinge on their approbation.

As a reporter, you will occasionally confront situations in which carrying out your professional responsibilities leaves you at odds with your personal feelings. The best response to that uneasiness arises from compassion.

The dictionary defines compassion as a feeling of deep sympathy for another's suffering or misfortune, accompanied by a desire to alleviate the pain or remove the cause.

People can detect genuine interest and concern. That is the key—overcome your discomfort and focus your concern on the person who has suffered.

There's no escaping it: To report, you must talk to the people involved. Often that involves interviewing people in abnormal circumstances. Who besides a reporter or a minister has a need to speak with people in such circumstances?

And the unusual circumstances are not confined to police stories. In a story involving women who started a career at midlife, a reporter I worked with interviewed a woman (who had remarried) whose first husband repeatedly told her he had castrated himself by doing housework so she could return to school. The reporter assumed that the former husband wouldn't want to discuss that unhappy time, so she didn't try to reach him. She confessed feeling ill at ease about trying to talk to him. But when contacted, the man was eager to talk and his comments were significant. It is a lesson not to be forgotten: Reach everyone who is central to the story—but especially those cast in a bad light.

BEWARE THE AX GRINDER

In most cities, there are enough factions to ensure that one or another will talk. Finding ax grinders is part of developing sources; it also is a point of professional peril.

Peril? What gives? You are supposed to develop sources and then you are told to watch out for them?

Exactly right. Just because someone in a position to know something tells you something doesn't make it true. Ax grinders have their own special reasons for telling. They do not want

their names attached to the dirty work, so they demand anonymity. Some reporters are willing to withhold the name of the
accuser because most times identifying the source would make
it obvious that the criticism is partisan sniping.

Some editors are not greatly concerned about going without
naming the sources. Nothing but the libel laws stand in your
way if the editors want it, but such stuff can quickly make you
appear to be partisan.

If you want to keep faith with the readers, print nothing that
is based only on the word of one source unless you can attribute the information to that source, by name, in the story.
(And you remember to ask, "How does this person know what
she or he is saying?")

And while we are talking of leveling with the readers, remember never to use a "composite" fictional person—not as a
source and not as a subject. The Janet Cooke fiasco at the
Washington Post with the imaginary child drug addict was
enough of that nonsense.

High standards will cause you to miss some stories—stories
that you are convinced need to be reported. Even so, it is a
mistake to trade integrity for expediency. Not even the most
trusted source should be published without someone or some
documents to support what is said.

Besides, there are skills that can, sometimes, make such com-
promises unnecessary.

First, do not quickly accept that sources won't go on the
record. Be patient and try to persuade them. Most of them
want the information put before the public. So cajole and
urge—work to convince them to attach their name to the report.

One acceptable way to get things into the paper is to have
supporting documents. Find public records that will either
give you what is needed or lead you to other supporting evidence.

A partial list includes: Motions filed in court, especially those that ask the court to seal part of the record; wills filed in probate court; search warrants and the returns showing what was found; applications to county tax appeal boards; license applications, from driver's license to bartending; depositions and affidavits, public audits, immigration and naturalization records and criminal records. Ask for travel vouchers, phone records, vendor files (records of business done with a firm filed by firm name), grant proposals and progress reports required by the federal government and consultant reports.

Know where records are stored. Get acquainted with the Freedom of Information Act; that includes federal and state provisions. But fighting over the FOI Act can be time-consuming and expensive. It is better, and quicker, to simply ask politely for documents than to fight.

Watch for names of corporations on business dealings. Nonprofit corporations must file forms (990) with the U.S. government that provide information on income, expenditures and other vital gore. Go to the secretary of state and learn the names of the officers and directors of a corporation. Learn, if you are stymied, the maiden names of wives of people involved; they are popular cover names for corporations. And never overlook the value of friendly, informed clerks. They often know whether some important or notorious figure has filed papers. If it is a rich family or a corporation, check to see whether they have created a charitable trust, which in most places requires a charter statement of purpose and reports on what has been done with the assets.

One of the most overlooked sources are U.S. marshals. Many of the restrictions placed on other court-supervised agents do not apply to them.

Look at land records. People form corporations for tax purposes, and names appear on deeds or mortgages filed with the assessor or county clerk. (Be aware that those who pay the taxes might not be the owners.) Three more public records to check: expense accounts, tax liens and minutes of public entities.

A reporter is seldom stuck with the word of just one source. If that happens, pause. Why believe the accuser? It is not enough that the information is juicy. Verify it or forget it.

A reporter should not be a prosecutor. (But there is nothing to prevent you going to the accused person and saying what you have heard. He or she might acknowledge the facts and give you what you need for publication—with attribution.) Don't give up, though. Good reporters have a powerful desire to get the information. Jeffrey Klein of *Mother Jones* says he knows he has a good story when he becomes obsessed. But be wary of obsessions—they can cause loss of perspective.

Match the fervor to know with a concern for fairness based on a full understanding of all that is pertinent. You can have lots of the facts, but still get things wrong if you don't understand *all* that they mean. Test your understanding; ask what other interpretations can be made from the same information.

Consider two stories that make the rounds occasionally in metropolitan areas. The first is an oldie: Children at Halloween get doctored candy or apples with razor blades or needles slipped into them.

The test for that is simple: Show me the apple or the doctored candy. Beyond that, show me the physicians who treated an injured child. Test the facts. A police report of a parent turning in an apple isn't good enough. Go to the parent, ask where it came from. Has the parent tried to find the culprit? (As a parent I can assure you that if my child received such a thing, I would hunt down the giver.) If the parent hasn't, pitch the allegation into the trash can. At the very least in checking these Halloween horror stories, don't publish until you talk to the victim or the parents.

More recently, a newspaper in the Upper Midwest reported that two junior high school girls were offered marijuana or cocaine for payment as baby-sitters. Apparently, the reporters did not find the students and ask who made the offers. The parents did not pursue the offenders. The paper published reports from school officials.

Why did parents let such matters stop short of prosecution? Why didn't the police press the case? It might all be true, but it also might be apocryphal.

IDENTIFYING SOURCES

Comes now the question of who is to know the identity of a source. The rule should be simple and safe for a reporter: If you tell me, you are telling my editor.

Right away you might think about Ben Bradlee not knowing (or saying he didn't know) the identity of "Deep Throat" in the Watergate reporting. What about that?

It was a mistake on Bradlee's part, and unnecessary. Perhaps if editor Bradlee had become involved more closely in testing reporter Woodward's information, he could have prevented the errors made in reporting that story.

The *Washington Post* served this country well in its reporting of Watergate. But it could have done just as well by avoiding the only-the-reporter-can-know approach—it is the approach that procured for Janet Cooke a Pulitzer Prize she couldn't keep.

It is bad practice to fly alone. Considering that the editor is responsible for lawsuits, I find it odd that his involvement is not required. Whatever, it is unnecessary.

Telling others increases the chance that the information will leak to people not needing to know. That concern is minor, however, compared to the importance of having others review the material provided. This involves assessing the source and the reasons for wanting the information known, and examining how the person came to know it. All these should be considered before an editor decides whether to publish the information.

There are dozens of questions that need to be asked when someone is providing damaging information. For one thing, how did the informant learn what he or she is telling you? Informants might well believe what they say is true, but lack access to other information that would show it to be otherwise. Sincerity is no assurance that sources have it right; the source could have been set up.

Testing information requires knowing the source's identity. The source who tells you he or she won't talk to anyone but you or refuses to let you share his or her identity with your editors is a source to try to convince. If you can't, forget the source. If he or she can't trust your judgment and that of your editors, why should there be trust from the other side? The temptation to run with something juicy will always be strong. Resist doing so without testing the information. Testing requires checking the source and his motives.

Beyond that, we have an obligation to let the readers know the source so they can judge what we know.

STAYING COOL

If ever there was a job that has frustration built in, it is reporting. We are paid to know and tell, but getting the information and understanding it can be very frustrating. When things reach a low point, be aware of your state of mind and do not lose your temper with news sources.

That is different from saying you should never display anger. Controlled anger can be a legitimate response. Applying controlled anger to achieve intimidation will occasionally get you information that otherwise might not be forthcoming.

I suppose a book of tips such as this should provide guidelines for when to try intimidation/anger and when not to. Sorry; I don't have any. You will have to judge when it will work and when it won't. I will say this: Use it sparingly. As I remarked earlier, you can move an elbow with a feather far easier than you can with a hammer. And it is more pleasant.

OBLIGATIONS TO NEWS SOURCES

Bob Scheer of the *Los Angeles Times* said he twice broke "off-the-record" agreements. The first was when Hubert Humphrey returned from Vietnam and said, off the record, that there had been proposals of peace from North Vietnam. The official line was that there had not been any offers.

The second occasion was when Scheer learned that during a dinner at the home of columnist-hostess Joan Braden, Nelson Rockefeller had proposed a toast to Richard Helms, stating, "We're with you no matter what you have done." What made it news, Scheer said, was that at the time Rockefeller was head of a commission investigating whether Helms had done any wrong as head of the CIA. The public's need to know those facts, Scheer felt, was stronger than his need to honor the off-the-record agreement with Braden. So he blew the whistle.

Questions of ethics require the best common sense and judgment you can bring to them. I agree with Scheer that a public person with power has no right that I would recognize to lie to the public in matters that affect the public directly. Distortions became part of U.S. policy in Vietnam. If you learn something of vital importance off the record and can prove it beyond doubt, the obligation to report transcends that of protecting a source's identity. Journalistic conventions, including those of abiding by agreements with news sources, are important. But there are not many occasions of equal importance to lying about Vietnam. Scheer saw a moral obligation that transcended the ethics of playing fair with a news source.

5

ADVICE TO THE STRIVER
(Murphy's Almanac for Farming
the Fourth Estate)

There was a time when people of breeding did not have to worry that their children would lust after jobs as reporters. If car wrecks and pregnancies were avoided, parents could hope their offspring might turn out well. But improved salaries and Watergate have made journalism more respectable and attractive.

The current myth is that no one goes into journalism for money. Power? Maybe, but not money. A fair number hew to journalism because they are writers, and journalists get paid to write. Others have always wanted to run something and what better than a newsroom?

Ambition is a common enough trait among the healthy and eager. More money, more respect, more power, more fun.

For the ambitious, let me provide an Almanac for Farming the Fourth Estate.

GETTING HIRED

First, you must get hired. Your best bet is to be born into the right family. Marriage should not be overlooked; many editors and publishers trace their success to marriage.

The next best way to get hired is to demonstrate you can do the work.

Start writing—for the high school or college newspaper, stringing for a daily, writing free lance. Of course, that means finding time to report and write without neglecting other studies. That was a problem for me. By your junior year in college you should get serious about collecting clippings. Think of them as evidence that you can find good stories and report and write them interestingly.

I started at 16 by providing statistics on high school football games and answering a rewrite man's questions over the phone. He wrote a short story using the statistics and highlights that I provided.

The next year, I produced stories to run in advance of games. I mimicked what I learned from reading. Having stood, I was allowed to walk; having walked, I earned the chance to run.

When I was drafted into the Army, I was assigned to a military newspaper because of my high school experience and college studies. By the time I returned to college, I had written everything from travel pieces to movie reviews. That experience led to a job as campus correspondent for the Topeka papers. My editor suggested stories and I volunteered some ideas of my own. All the time, my goal was to learn my craft, gain experience and gather clips that demonstrated my skills.

I knew my plan was working when a story of mine in the student paper produced a job offer. The story involved a phenomenal football halfback who transferred to the University of Kansas. He lost his eligibility for violating NCAA rules, but not before he dazzled the Big 8 conference with his power and speed.

I and everyone else knew an NCAA ruling on his eligibility was coming, but I got an edge by planning. The evening a ruling was due, I called his apartment and hit it lucky. He had just received the bad news. I got an exclusive interview, which was published simultaneously with the announcement of his being declared ineligible.

It was *the* sports story in the state, and every sports editor in Kansas would have run it. I chose to let my school paper break it first, and though that caused some grumbling, the story helped establish me as someone who could compete. I had clips. Now, the area papers knew my work.

Some people call it paying your dues. I think of it as learning your craft. There is a difference. You can pay your dues and not learn your craft. Putting in your time is not enough; you must learn.

The best way to get hired by a daily newspaper after finishing college is to have a summer internship at a daily newspaper. The best way to get an internship is to have clippings accumulated while in college. Mix those things with a solid academic record and you are in the running.

College placement personnel might have useful suggestions for finding work. Whatever else, you must find a job reporting and, I repeat, learn your craft. Seek opportunities to get good stories. Write them interestingly and carefully. Then contact those you would work for and show them your work.

In the years that I screened reporter applications, I was struck by how many said, "I'll take any job." I know that is a recommended strategy—take any job because once inside you have a better chance of getting the job you want. It might work, but it is poor business, for both the newspaper and the candidate. You learn your craft by practicing it—not as a clerk but as a reporter. Go to the reporting jobs.

Many aspirants refuse to serve an apprenticeship in a small town. They overlook the advantages of working for a smaller daily.

Foremost, at a smaller paper you can report many different beats and stories. Try it all—city government, courts, budgets, police, disasters, agriculture. You can do sports features even if you know little of sports. Write profiles.

But however you do it, find an apprenticeship. Work as a reporter, not as a clerk. Free lance feature writing is better than nothing after college, but just barely.

If you are unwilling or unable to serve your apprenticeship, my counsel is not going to be very helpful in getting you a regular newspaper job.

Most people set the curve of their careers in the first three to five years. It is then they acquire the habits that will make or break them.

If you get an apprenticeship, bury yourself in your work. Try covering everything. Think of it as graduate school with pay.

Work three to five years learning to report and write before you aim at the top. Collect your eight or ten best clips and start your search.

Several stories of quality are more valuable than a string-book bulging with nothing stories. Try to make certain that a story has a chance to be a winner before you invest lots of time. But whatever your approach, clippings are the rungs on the job ladder. It will be tough to climb without them.

Give some thought to your clipping folder. Get a good, clean print of each story and trim the ragged edges and paste it straight on a clean page, one clipping per page.

Some editors wonder how the reporter got the story. Was it presented on a platter or did it require initiative? Did it need extensive rewriting? Was it written on deadline? Short explanations typed beside the clipping can add a nice touch.

As for a résumé, keep it to two pages maximum. Below is part of mine:

Résumé

Terence Patrick Murphy
726 Mentor Road
Minneapolis, Minnesota 67530
682-384-6910

Married, two children
6 ft., 185 lbs.
Born March 3, 1936
Sedalia, Missouri

Business experience: (Include other jobs when you lack newspaper experience.)

March 1977—present: Minneapolis Tribune. Assignments editor for morning and Sunday paper. Direct politics and government reporting. 245,000 a.m.; 600,000 Sunday.

Miscellaneous: Taught advanced reporting at University of Kansas during 1971-72 school year. Started reporting as stringer for sports in high school. Sports editor of Korean edition of *Pacific Stars & Stripes* while in Army.

Worked for United Press International in Kansas City, Missouri, senior year in college, reporting general assignment and Kansas City Athletics.

Worked to finance last two years of high school and all of college.

Education: Started at Kansas State University at Manhattan in 1954. After Army service, finished B.S. in journalism at the University of Kansas at Lawrence in 1963.

Honors: Student Council president, Manhattan (Kansas) High School, 1954. Junior class president. State winner Elks Youth Leadership Contest, and runnerup national contest.

Interests: Writer of fiction, professional books; manager of young girls softball team; avid reader; enjoy tennis, golf, fishing, hunting.

References: John Jones, managing editor, Maintown Gazette, 1900 Main Street, Maintown, Kansas 66044

That is one common résumé form. Proofread it for neatness and typographical errors.

Once you have your clips and résumé prepared, pick the paper or papers you want to work for. The *Editor & Publisher Year Book,* which can be found in many libraries, lists essential information about newspapers in your immediate region and outside it. Before you send your application, call the city desk during a slack time. For morning papers, try late morning or early afternoon; for afternoon papers, try between 2:30 and 4 P.M. Identify yourself as a reporter and ask to whom clips and résumés should be mailed. Do not be discouraged by suggestions that no one is being hired. Two weeks later, call the person you sent the clips to. You are now into salesmanship and you must feel your way.

Persistence can be important, but you can overdo it. No editor needs to be driven crazy. (Many are half crazed already.)

If you are told they like your clips but there are no openings, keep in touch by sending fresh clips and include a letter telling what you are doing professionally. Keep a record of correspondence.

GETTING AHEAD

Now that you've landed a job, here are other things to keep in mind:

If you want to be managing editor or editor, you need to cover city hall, state government, politics or Washington. Sooner is better than later. William Allen White of the *Emporia Gazette* in Kansas called politics an editor's meat and potatoes. Most big-paper editors dined at the political table as reporters.

Newspapers promote reporters who are familiar with how politicians operate. Power makes news for any newspaper, and politicians hold the levers of power. Certainly, they play games to get power and keep it. Reporters near them learn things that the family living editor has no chance to learn. Here's another tip:

Don't get pegged as a feature writer if someday you want to run the newsroom. Editors love to rave about their best and brightest writers, but it is the bright reporter who gets promoted to editor and managing editor. (Not that reporters can't or shouldn't write well.)

Newsroom editors supervise reporters, and because reporters are more respectful of bosses who have been there, it makes sense to pick reporters over feature writers or copy editors for supervisors. Almost every good newspaper emphasizes reporting above writing. You can damn that practice or praise it, but be aware of it.

The Knight-Ridder newspaper chain is said to have this view: Every reporter gets beaten during his career; editors are reporters who were beaten the least often. Yes, that translates into aggressiveness; but it need not mean abrasive or rude. You can work your way to the front without excessive arm waving and toe trampling.

No matter where you begin, learn the fundamentals of reporting. In addition, know that each newsroom has its conventions. Don't worry about them, but be alert to them, particularly when you are the new reporter.

Advising reporters to learn their craft might seem out of place in a chapter dealing with ambition. It is not. Ambition is free; all it takes is the desire.

To fulfill ambition you need to set yourself apart from the pack. Consider the advice of Pulitzer Prize-winner Seymour Hersh: "I spent a winter in Pierre, South Dakota, covering the Legislature . . . you should do it."

Hersh also praises his experiences in working at the City News Bureau in Chicago, covering crime news. He speaks of learning the basics of the craft.

Dust the glitter from the jacket of Seymour Hersh, and you find a reporter dedicated to competence and preparation. It is reassuring to hear Hersh tell an audience of journalists, "Our influence has been profound." More important is his advice not to "worry about being negative . . . worry about being wrong."

James Polk, who won a Pulitzer at the *Washington Star* for exposing illegal campaign contributions, thinks the greatest threat to reporting is not libel damages or those who chip away at the Freedom of Information Act. The greatest threats are

laziness, carelessness and the failure of reporters to practice
with dedication the basics, the drudgery, that allow them to
report with certain accuracy.

Polk and Hersh are two of the most admired reporters in
American journalism. One tells us that there are no shortcuts
to good reporting; the other talks of serving time in Pierre,
South Dakota, and on the police beat. You must pay your dues,
learn your trade, if you want to emulate their careers. Going to
South Dakota might be extreme; working the police beat is not.

There is no substitute for developing the skills that make a
reporter a journeyman. Cover the crime beat, the courts, state
government; offer to substitute for beat reporters on vacations.

You might get away with being a less than scintillating writer. But know from day one that you cannot get beaten by the
competition day after day and still move upward. Newspaper
owners want editors and reporters who know how to get stories from the basic beats. The fundamental job of a newspaper
is gathering news and reporting it clearly.

It happens occasionally that a bright young star is spotted
and taken away from reporting. The advice here is stay with
reporting. Too many good reporters get diverted too soon. At
the better papers, the leaders did their time in the reporting
trenches.

Of course, if you aspire to editing or don't enjoy reporting,
follow your own counsel. Copy editors have been and will be
promoted. But if you want to play the odds, you learn to be a
journeyman reporter first.

Don't wear your ambition like an armband. Work hard, tell the
boss what you aspire to do and then produce the best you can.
And realize that you just might not get what you want when
you want it. As Mick Jagger said in another context, you can't
always get what you want, but you might get what you need.

There is no magic to be learned that works wonders for your
career. Anything you can pull from a hat nice and easy is bound
to be tricky. Instead, you should identify the fundamentals of

reporting and learn them through practice. A beat is a good place for learning. But whatever your assignments remember this: *You advance your career if you do well at whatever your job is.* (If only the impatient eager beavers recognized that.) That means you make the most of each assignment. Concentrate on the opportunity at hand rather than fret about not being on the main line to the top. Be thorough and learn what precision means.

You best serve ambition by finding and writing stories that literally walk onto the front page. This requires thought, planning, work, and learning how to pack a story with useful information in a form that is compelling to read.

Don't confuse titles with advancement. Recognize the difference between assistant editor and assistant to the editor. One has her or his own domain; the other runs errands. Seek positions with responsibility and authority.

Another thing: Those of you propelled by ambition need to have principles that you hold as convictions, and act on them. Be a free person, first; and then a person of conscience, and so on down the line. You need principles other than those of ambition to guide you. Don't whine. Do your part. Learn to let your work be an escape from other cares and worries.

ON TIME AND OVERTIME

I have always been impressed by people who never arrive at work on time. Not in a positive way, but impressed nonetheless. Some bosses might not care about that. But tardiness can affect productivity. If you have a problem getting your copy in on time, start work earlier.

Some ask why being fifteen minutes late is a big deal. What's fifteen minutes? Well, maybe it is nothing. But if it is nothing, try to arrive fifteen minutes early every workday for a month.

That might give you a different perspective.

The basic point is that you shouldn't chisel. There is no good reason to make being late a habit. And if you start work at a place where you see others arriving late and taking leisurely lunches, hold off on joining in. Be certain it isn't a courtesy extended only to veterans. *Earn a privilege before you use it.*

The laws governing most jobs require that you be paid time-and-a-half for work performed in any week in which you have already worked forty hours. In most states, you cannot be required to work overtime without being paid. You can be required to work overtime, however.

Generally, you will need permission in advance when you want to work overtime. Here are a couple of occasions when it might be wise to ask for overtime:

1. When with overtime you can get a good story into the next edition.
2. When you can talk with someone vital to the story who otherwise would be difficult to reach.

Be reasonable about overtime. Whether you should turn in every fifteen minutes is doubtful. But when you work a half hour or more, keep track of it. File for it. You are entitled. Be leery of bosses who want you to take compensating time off later, but who don't keep precise records of time worked.

DEADLINES AND EDITIONS

Learn the deadlines for the different editions. If you are covering a night meeting, let the night supervisor know when you will be calling in. Prepare background material that can be in type before deadline. Some places call it "A matter," others "10 add."

You should tell the editor of a development even if the last deadline has passed. Sometimes presses don't start on time or editors choose to produce a "makeover" to allow part of an edition to carry a story. The point is to let your editor decide.

COLLEAGUES

From your first day in any newsroom, you will be working with others. Many reporters discover that those they work with make good friends outside the office too. Certainly, journalists understand the problems of journalists.

As a rookie or a newcomer, assume your lowest possible profile. Allow time to become known and take the time to know people as individuals. Emphasize listening. Your associations can bring you grief or an abundance of good things.

If you find a newsroom divided into warring camps, keep your focus where it belongs—outside the newsroom, out where the news is happening.

OFFICE POLITICS

Some try to travel to the top by taking the shortcut marked "office politics." Some make it. And it will be rare to find any who succeed by angering their superiors. But if your inclination is to succeed by politics, drop this book and pick up Machiavelli's 1513 classic, *The Prince*.

We all have only so much time and energy. The amount spent on office politics can't be used practicing your craft. Concentrate on doing work that can be admired by all.

I am not suggesting that you can or should ignore politics. But avoid being mean-spirited and petty. Read the bulletin board; don't post nasty comments unless you sign your name.

And remember that leaders come and go.

STYLE

Some people go crazy trying to figure which "personal style" is most admired by the bosses.

Sadly, style seems to matter more than it should. More and more of the jokes that used to be told about junior executives at IBM and Procter & Gamble can be told of the "news managers" of the big chains. How are they picked? Compatibility and predictability seem to be big items. (Which might explain why so many chain editors produce predictable, boring newspapers.)

Whatever, recognize that life is filled with little trades. The best advice is to relax and be yourself. The better editors recognize examples of first-rate reporting and those displays will overcome many shortcomings of "style."

BECOMING A HACK

I'm not certain what the word "hack" means to most persons, but to me a hack journalist is someone who is careless about checking information and who perceives many stories to be much alike. Several years doing the same jobs can dull any reporter's senses.

Perhaps the surest way to become a hack newspaper reporter is, day after day, to base your sense of worth on the volume of your work. Production *is* important. But anyone can report routine events of government and fill a clip book. In fact, most hack reporters have.

A hack reporter talks with the same limited list of sources. When passed through the eyes and ears of a hack, one government story reads much like all other government stories. The hack seldom provides an explanation of the events or circumstances that led to an action. And it is rare for a hack to try to explain how a program will work in detail—how it will affect people outside city government.

The hack takes the handout or the prepared statement and pumps it into the newspaper without trying to help people understand what difference any of it might make. To the hack, all of reporting and most of writing is a series of replays—a redoing of things done before.

The remedy is to work at keeping an eternally fresh eye and ear.

Always pull the clips from the newspaper's library. If your notes are not clear, call your sources again. Check your information. Use the library for other references. Be wary of shortcuts and don't rely on your memory too much.

If you are covering a beat, vary your routine—spend time with middle-level bureaucrats. They know the history of the place and can offer useful perspectives.

Do not make assumptions. For instance, it would be a mistake to assume that everyone in an anti-abortion organization is conservative.

Routines that translate into thoroughness are valuable—such as always asking people for the proper spelling of their names. But you are pouring the footings for becoming a hack when routines take the place of fresh thinking and listening.

No one ever consciously decided to become a hack. But it can happen—unless you stay alert.

STRESS AND STRAIN

One person's joy in competition is another's stress. What is a lively exchange of views for some is a personal attack for others. Feelings come into play in newsrooms.

If bad feelings dominate your professional life, ask yourself what you expect from your work and from those with whom you associate. Much of your work climate will always be beyond your control, but not beyond your influence. What you do and how you do it can matter.

Be forgiving and acquire perspective. Time does heal—not all things, maybe, but almost all.

Learn to express your feelings and thoughts in an easy and open manner. If you store your anger and nurse it into a full-blown grudge, you buy trouble for yourself and others. Deal with the substance of a conflict, even when it requires that you have to work your way through personality differences.

One of the most unheralded cures for woes is not to dwell on them. Get busy rather than fret. Got a problem you can't do anything to change? Then turn to doing other things—constructive things. Acquire new skills; stretch yourself professionally and keep trying.

And while I am treating you to knee-side lectures, remember the dangers of drink. Some reporters like to relax and socialize over a drink. Some drink at lunch. Which raises at least one question: Who of sound mind would try to do serious work after drinking? Wait at least until your work is done.

Do you find you have trouble unwinding at bedtime? Instead of taking sleeping pills, take yourself outside. Walk a bit, jog a bit; make yourself sleepy nature's way.

Tension is a fact of contemporary life and we have to deal with it. Remember to laugh and include yourself on the list of what you laugh at.

YOUR FAMILY

"How are things going for you?" To me that has always meant how did I like my work; how did my family and I like where we lived; and how is my health and that of my family?

Although there is a limit to what a supervisor or employer should be asked to accommodate, nearly every paper recognizes that personal matters can become matters of first importance. When you have to deal with a problem, tell your supervisor.

Remember that you read it here: Don't neglect your home life. That means you balance your job and your family. It doesn't mean you can't find time to throw yourself into your work. *Just remember to rotate your enthusiasm.*

BEING TREATED FAIRLY

Everyone has a stake in fairness and equity in a newsroom. People who work hard and meet high standards are entitled to job security, decent treatment and the best wage possible. Be aware that many of the benefits you enjoy on your first day on the job were earned by union members. Respect the price paid by those who went through strikes (if there have been strikes) and respect the time invested in negotiating for the benefits you enjoy. Learn how the union works, study the contract, attend meetings. Pay your dues, literally and figuratively.

For fun and some insight into union origins, read the laborers' anthem:

Solidarity Forever!

By Ralph Chaplin

(Tune: "Battle Hymn of the Republic")

When the Union's inspiration through the workers' blood shall run,
There can be no power greater anywhere beneath the sun.
Yet what force on earth is weaker than the feeble strength of one?
But the Union makes us strong.

Chorus:

Solidarity forever!
Solidarity forever!
Solidarity forever!
For the Union makes us strong.

Is there aught we hold in common with the greedy parasite
Who would lash us into serfdom and would crush us with his might?
Is there anything left for us but to organize and fight?
For the Union makes us strong.

Chorus

It is we who plowed the prairies; built the cities where they trade;
Dug the mines and built the workshops; endless miles of railroad laid.
Now we stand outcasts and starving, 'mid the wonders we have made;
But the Union makes us strong.

Chorus

All the world that's owned by idle drones is ours and ours alone.
We have laid the wide foundations; built it skyward stone by stone.
It is ours, not to slave in, but to master and to own,
While the Union makes us strong.

Chorus

They have taken untold millions that they never toiled to earn.
But without our brain and muscle not a single wheel can turn.
We can break their haughty power; gain our freedom when we learn
That the Union makes us strong.

Chorus

In our hands is placed a power greater than their hoarded gold;
Greater than the might of armies, magnified a thousand-fold.
We can bring to birth the new world from the ashes of the old,
For the Union makes us strong.

6

EDITORS AND THE NEWSROOM

Good editors have several common qualities, starting with clear ideas, news judgment and the ability to articulate what they want to deliver to their readers. Add to that a consistent, predictable method for getting the work done and you have an editor who ranks among the very best. Such editors maintain two-way communications with the reporters and other editors. Everyone on the staff has a clear sense of priorities.

The worst supervising editors place no value on building and maintaining a functional staff organization. They see themselves as *artistes* whose style must not be shackled by proven ways of doing business. The editors who work for such "leaders" are inevitably frustrated and often become spreaders of the disease. Just as clearly stated purposes and known responsibilities can make things work, disorganization produces frustration and burned-out staff members who constantly check the gauges to see which way the boss is blowing. The editor who fancies himself a one-person show seldom allows the newsroom managers to be much more than conductors of heat from those above to those below.

However, important as they are, management skills are no substitute for news judgment. If your editor lacks judgment, he can't produce much of a paper. Sooner or later he will divert the resources toward the wrong places.

Count it as good news in your first days at a newspaper if you see evidence that the editor and the managing editor read the newspaper, cover to cover, every day. Editors can say they care, but nothing makes the point better than short notes attached to clips, which sing praises or pinpoint shortcomings—passed along through your supervising editor. An editor who does not measure success by what is published fails to measure the paper the way the reader measures it—by reading it.

But some of the worst editors to work for also read the newspaper closely, every day. The problem is in the way they channel comments. They send notes directly to reporters praising what is published without knowing whether it took heroic work by editors, and, similarly, finding fault without knowing who might be responsible. (Producing a story involves more than reporting and writing. Editing is important. On the experimental newspaper *PM* in New York City during the 1940s, each reporter was his own editor—meaning there was no editor. It didn't work.)

The very worst editors cannot wait to deliver their thunderbolts. They do not ask why something was done or not done and they offer judgments rather than explain what is to be learned from the error.

Comments from a variety of critics confuse reporters and copy editors as to who must be pleased. The best-run shops have a clear chain of command. If you are working where you need worry only about your immediate supervisor, you are fortunate.

That is the essence of staff organization. It should delineate responsibilities and authority. The worst places give responsibilities but skimp on the authority needed to do the work. *You need one person from whom you can get your questions answered and receive your directions.*

KEEP YOUR EDITOR INFORMED

Whatever management condition prevails, learn what is expected. Do not be a reporter whom the editors have to pump to find out how a story is progressing. Call in regularly when away from the office; check your mailbox for messages; keep the secretaries informed of where you can be reached. Why? Sources might have called to tell you they cannot make an appointment, or spot news might be breaking near where you are. Unless you are wearing a beeper, the desk cannot reach you. And when you are out of town or even in an outlying suburb, call before you head back to the office. You might be able to check out a fire or an accident on the way in.

SHAPING COPY

For many reporters, the editors who shape copy are the most trying of colleagues. A good editor can improve almost any copy. But how does one recognize a good editor?

Journalism is often a matter of taste. It can be a very arbitrary business: Something is good because someone declares it to be. Recognize that there are many "right" ways to tell any story. You are fortunate if you work with an editor who also recognizes that. *Pray to get an editor who is consistent and who can articulate the qualities that he or she thinks are missing.* The worst will leave their fingerprints on virtually every line you write.

For your part, recognize that nobody's copy is always exactly right. All of us can be aided by editing. The trick is to accept good editing and to display patience and courtesy in dealing with editors. Recognize that copy editors are hired to challenge copy and help get the facts straight.

But what should you do when you and your editor come to a dead-end dispute in editing copy? *Seek the compromise—create*

*the attractive alternative. Try rewriting to meet the editor's re-
quirements in a form you can accept. Do not let ego overwhelm the
process.*

There are lots of "right" ways to do things. Be bright enough
to know that it doesn't always have to be *your* "right" way. All
of us have just so much energy to spend. Pick your spots.

When your copy is helped or saved by the alertness of others, write a note of appreciation.

Some editors wait until the story has been written to offer
their views on how it should be done. Such a nonconsultive
approach can be O.K. If your stories sail through without extensive work, let the system be.

However, if important elements are added or the focus of a
story is commonly changed, try consulting while the writing is
in progress. That allows converting second guessing into first
guessing. Start by discussing the scope of the story, what it is
expected to tell readers, how much time is needed to produce
it and how long it should be. You can extend this consultive
approach to the reporting. There should be conversations if
the scope changes or the story changes in emphasis.

HOW YOUR WORK IS JUDGED

All of us can stand a kind word now and again. On the other
hand, if all your work wins praise, you are working for a friendly person but not one who can help you learn through unadorned, critical appraisals.

Declare yourself fortunate if you work for professionals who
know the difference between good work and bad and respond
accordingly. The best bosses deliver good news with a smile
and less-good news in a calm manner.

The way you receive criticism will affect the way it is deliv-
ered. It is a bit like the way a prudent person approaches a
swinging door. If someone is on the other side, poised to block

your entry, you go at it one way. On the other hand, if you expect someone to help you open that door, or at least not resist the opening, a gentler approach can be anticipated.

Some reporters are happier not hearing specific assessments of their work. They make one hell of a mistake. The criticism doesn't go away; it just moves beyond their hearing. And by being less than open to questions, reporters lose the opportunity to explain why certain things were done, or not done.

Every reporter gets a job review. It can show up in negative ways, in missed merit pay and promotions. You need to understand your shortcomings. How else can you learn what skills your bosses think you need to develop? If no formal system for evaluations exists, ask for details of what you need to work on.

Whether your boss provides formal evaluations or not, you should and can grade your own work. A checklist:

Do your stories consistently earn good display? If not, ask whether the reason is something you are doing or failing to do.

Do you show initiative in going after stories and in thinking of possible stories?

Do you keep track of front-page stories for later developments? Why not follow them? You already have an understanding of the elements of these stories. Readership studies show a strong interest in stories that keep track of a person or an event.

Do you make many "little" mistakes—misspellings, sloppy copy? Work to clean them up. No one wants to pick up your journalistic room.

Do you meet deadlines? Ask how you might improve.

Add skills and work on weaknesses. But also make full use of the skills you have. There is no fairer measure of discipline than that. It takes a dedicated professional to deliver those skills every day on every story.

A journeyman remembers how easy it is to get things wrong.

That is why precision is so important. Get the details right. Listen carefully. Check your copy before turning it in.

UNWANTED ASSIGNMENTS

Consciously or unconsciously, almost every assignment editor remembers reporters according to something that few journalism textbooks talk about—the unwanted assignment.

I am not suggesting that you greet each assignment with the same degree of enthusiasm. If you have compelling reasons for not doing the story, state them. But if you still must do it, be a professional. Don't kiss off an assignment with halfhearted efforts. It can become a habit.

You can drag your feet on unwanted assignments, doing just the minimum, but there is a price attached to that. Over the long haul, that attitude brings its own rewards. They are not the same rewards given for hard work.

Gay Talese, in his book on *The New York Times*, titled *The Kingdom and the Power*, tells how one reporter, Harrison Salisbury, dealt with an apparently uninspiring assignment on his return to New York after five years in Moscow. Says Talese:

[In a bureau] One is not surrounded by so many editors . . . he enjoys long stretches of freedom, writing and moving about as he wishes. All this stops when the correspondent returns, as Salisbury did in 1954, to the home office. . . . His final assignment for the foreign desk, a series of articles on Russia that he had written shortly after arriving back in New York (and that would win for him the Pulitzer in 1955), made Salisbury quite famous. . . . Yet some editors . . . indulged in a procedure that no longer persists at *The Times* but was then quite common: they would level Salisbury a bit, bring him down to earth.

The first assignment . . . was about trash and garbage . . . a recurring assignment . . . revived almost every time that [the publisher's

wife] returned from Europe. [The assignment arose from her] interest
in such things as parks and in a cleaner New York. (Most reporters
dispensed with them in less than an hour and could be done in six
paragraphs.)

When Salisbury got this assignment . . . his reaction was sudden: he
would turn this into the biggest trash-and-garbage story in the history
of *The New York Times.* And he did . . . it became a three-part series
that started on page one.

Harrison Salisbury got an unwanted assignment. He made
the most of it.

But reasonableness should work both ways. If you detect after several months that the least desirable assignments go to
those who resist them the least, point that out to your supervisor. (Raw rookies should do the work and be silent.)

But whatever you do, remember that you leave your brand
on all the work you do, not just what you enjoy. Reporters who
do good work on stories they themselves suggest, but do no-
ticeably less well on those assigned to them, are begging trouble. The trouble might come not in the form of punishment,
but as denied opportunities.

"MY EDITOR WANTS . . ."

Another habit worth developing is to deal with the idea rather
than with the source of the idea. Some reporters resist a
change in copy or an assignment, but acquiesce when they
hear: "The M.E. wants it." If it is a horse-manure idea, it remains a horse-manure idea even if the M.E. wants it.

Deal with the idea. If it is truly stupid, state your reasons as
specifically and unemotionally as you can; offer alternatives
that will meet the need. You are off course when you are
tempted to ask, "Whose idea is it?"

There might be times when an editor insists that you pursue
an angle or ask a question not to your liking. When the ques-

tion makes you uncomfortable, there is a temptation to tell the source, "My editor wants me to ask . . ."

That is a mistake. It labels you as an errand runner and the source gets the notion that you don't give a damn about the subject or the question. That perception can cause the source to respond with a similar lack of candor and conviction.

Understand the question, state your reservations to the editor, and then ask it the way you would if it were your own.

COMPLAINTS AND END RUNS

If you have troubles with your boss, stay cool while seeking remedies. No single formula guarantees relief. And do not react until you have lived with the trouble awhile. It might go away.

Start by recognizing that a perfectly smooth relationship with an editor might very well be dangerous to your development. Just as most of us can get along with someone who is asleep, most reporters can get along with a supervisor who does not supervise. Some nonsupervisors are even embraced by the troops and held to be jolly good persons.

You are working for a kindly uncle or kindly aunt if you are never asked to do anything you don't want to do or if you are never diverted from something you are interested in. *Supervising, on occasion, means requiring all those things.*

Some reporters respond to unwanted assignments or changes in their copy by cranking up the end run—going over their bosses' heads—in search of relief. It might work. If it does, write this down: The place is run by poor managers.

If you have a complaint about how your copy has been edited or if you thoroughly dislike an assignment, start with your supervisor. Tell the "guilty" party of your feelings in as non-threatening a manner as possible. If that fails to produce improvement, take it one step at a time and be certain to tell your immediate supervisor that you intend to appeal. Your best move would be to invite the person to join you as you appeal.

Support your supervisor every way you can. Keep him informed. Learn those things he might have to teach you. Realize that the closer you work with an editor, as with anybody, the more vivid the warts. Familiarity is said to breed contempt. Among the people who seek solutions, familiarity will breed understanding.

But what do you do when you are hitched to a boss you can't tolerate? Perhaps union members or an older reporter can help with advice. If worse comes to worst, there is the door. Extreme cases might make it wise to seek remedy in the courts (such as with illegal discrimination).

GO TO HELL

There comes, into the lives of some, the occasional horse's rear end. Not all who are in charge are reasonable, and some who are unreasonable are also lacking in essential talents. To be stuck with that is no fun.

Edward Barrett, former dean of the Columbia University Graduate School of Journalism, has suggested that you save 10 percent of each paycheck to finance a Go-to-Hell Fund. That way, if you are stuck in an untenable situation, you will have the money to go elsewhere.

Take his advice. Save the money. But give the job a chance. If it just doesn't work, get yourself another job, and depart with a smile. Having money saved will make the move easier.

CONCLUSION:
Report the Human Experience

Virtually every newspaper has traditions of some sort that will affect you as a new reporter. The traditions of papers can be as different in their splendid state of monopoly as they were during the days of competition. Some survived by being sensational. Others triumphed by being less partisan and more alert to the need to write clearly and intelligently.

Whatever the traditions, you, as a professional, need to understand whom you serve. The romantic notion is that a journalist serves the public first, last and always. The extent to which the notion of journalism as a public service is laughed at where you work is the extent to which you work for money changers.

The simple truth is that public service is the only focus that can justify the special standing granted the press by the First Amendment. Some newspaper owners love that freedom but do not accept the sacred trust that goes with it.

With too many, the sacred trust has become a sacred cow that they milk to fill ever larger buckets. Too often they act as if the press had no obligations that could not be met by producing special advertising sections.

Exactly what newspapers should provide the public makes for soul-searching debates. In 1947, a group called the Hutchins Commission set forth an outline worth considering in its report, A *Free and Responsible Press.* Employing an incredibly dull and dry style, it stated that the press should provide:

1. A truthful, comprehensive and intelligent account of the day's events in a context which gives them meaning.
2. A forum for the exchange of comment and criticism.
3. The projection of a representative picture of the constituent groups in the society.
4. The presentation and clarification of the goals and values of the society.
5. Full access to the day's intelligence.

Time was when a country editor such as William Allen White could gain national prominence through his hard-hitting, brightly uttered editorials. White's editorials won a Pulitzer Prize; they also swayed votes and pulled politicians to his door. In those days, readers often were isolated, and they expected wisdom as well as information from editors. White was a window of understanding on a world far removed from those who bought his paper.

The readers of the *Emporia Gazette* in 1927, however, were quite different from today's readers—in Emporia or in New York City. They generally lacked education, often were very poor, and knew little by firsthand experience that went on beyond their county. Charles Lindbergh had just become the first person to fly solo across the Atlantic. Today men orbit the earth and have visited the moon. Travel is common, and education is widespread. William Allen White's audience no longer exists.

The spread of education has produced an explosion of information in specialties that burgeon overnight. In electronics alone there are more special interest readers (and magazines galore to serve them) than ever subscribed to Mr. White's *Emporia Gazette.*

But one thing that has not changed is the need for information to be edited—that is, put into a coherent, focused presentation.

That is a basic function of the newspaper—to provide focused information. Although our reporting must not be presented in a way that tries to do the thinking for the readers, it must be in a context that provides information that can be readily understood.

If done right, it allows different readers to draw different conclusions from the same information.

As important as serious reporting is for newspapers, the knowledge and expertness required to do it threaten to turn us into narrow professionals who are mesmerized by our research. Writing an analysis of current economic theory is a long way from the reporting of a murder or the aftermath of pain suffered by a family involved in tragedy. If too many reporters regard that difference as the gap between "good" journalism (read that sophisticated) and "bad" (read that old-fashioned), newsrooms could easily become isolated from all human activity except that of the cerebrum.

It is a mistake for a reporter to become increasingly removed from the world. I am referring to those aspects of the world that are very basic and direct—the world defined by the daily concerns of us all, rich and poor. It has to do with food, shelter, transportation, education, religion, recreation, work, illnesses, births, deaths, tragedies and triumphs and ever so many other human experiences. People care about these things and need to see how they affect individuals as well as their impact in a larger context. On this depends the cohesiveness of our society. Reporters who write on specialized subjects add greatly to the public understanding. But they shouldn't overlook the great variety of "unimportant" events that tell what life is like in a community.

The very size of our organizations can be a problem. Newspapers once were produced by printers working from a shirt-tail filled with type. Most journalists work for corporations and could not operate without them. But big buildings and better salaries can remove journalists from huge chunks of the public. Add the guards at the door at the typical big-city newspaper, and we are further insulated from those who lack a PR person to plead their cause.

There was a time as recently as the 1950s when papers were dominated by human interest stories, and the balance provided by intelligent reporting was needed. But the shift in the balance threatens to keep us ignorant of the common man's life.

Another, more recent influence that can affect the reporter has been the rise of the chains. There are good chains and bad, but the simple truth is that all chains are run from headquarters outside the communities the papers are supposed to serve. Editors can bow their necks to serve their communities, but the top managers, the people in charge, are far more concerned with topping last year's earnings than with carrying out the responsibilities of a free press. Few publishers of chain-owned papers get fired for poor editorial quality. Not so with those who consistently fail to top the previous year's profits.

Almost uniformly, papers taken over by chains show at least these immediate changes: better design and graphics, and higher advertising and circulation rates. Soon thereafter, there will be a growing dullness in the editorials, and a strong reluctance to rock the local boat.

And how do dull editorials harm the republic? The problem is that editorials tend to reflect the thinking of the management. The timid and the bland make poor watchdogs. Color photos are nice and no wise publisher would ignore the value of clean design and arresting graphics. But those are qualities you could find in newspapers published in countries ruled by military juntas—Argentina, for example.

Scrutinizing public officials is an American press tradition worth preserving. In most towns where chains operate, the merchants who make the chains rich are those who would like to influence public institutions to work to their advantages. That includes the bodies that set property values used for determining taxes, and it also includes those who have the power to grant zoning and use permits. These bodies even have the power to take property through condemnation.

So where does that leave you, the individual professional, if you work for a chain paper? Be assured that you will not change the thinking of a chain's managers. But also be assured that even in the most profit-minded newspaper, you can report important stories on sensitive matters. Concentrate on what you can get in the paper rather than on what you can't.

And do not make the mistake of assuming that a story won't be published. Do the reporting, write the story, and offer it as if it were routine. Of course, if important stories are blocked at every corner, you dip into the Go-to-Hell Fund and find work where managers will permit you to practice journalism.

As you practice journalism, keep in mind the point I have made throughout this book—that it is easier to serve as a conduit of information than it is to understand your material well enough to help the reader. "Neutrality" can intrude. Michael J. Kirkhorn, in a February 1982 *Quill* magazine essay titled "The Virtuous Journalist," asks whether the postures we maintain to avoid becoming partisans are not leaving us unable to understand the experiences we try to report. If we are totally detached, can we help readers understand what those who experience the event understand?

Detachment has been drummed into our heads as the foundation stone of fairness. But does that produce "fairness" or just something cold, removed and divorced from the real world that we hope to help our readers understand?

Robert Capa advised other war photographers to move closer if they wanted to improve their pictures. I recommend that you get close to the world that you would write about. Establish and maintain a professional distance so that your reporting can be full and balanced, but don't place yourself too far be-hind the front lines. Premature distancing is fatal to under-standing.

You cannot, will not, write the same way about something you understand as you will about something you experience in the abstract. If you do not care enough about a subject to un-derstand it, you cannot write about it so that others will care.

None of this should make the king of Gonzo journalists, Hunter Thompson, an acceptable model for newspaper writ-ing. Nor does it imply that experiencing things guarantees un-derstanding. But experiencing can help.

Bright writing that does not inform tries to entertain. We want to provide some entertainment, to be sure, because life itself is funny and newspapers should reflect a full picture. But the core of our work should be matters of consequence in the lives of people, and presented in a compelling, honest manner.

That should include reporting the need to grieve after a death as well as reporting the effect of the latest tax bills on the readers. Mixed among our grand pretensions, which are impor-tant, are the manageable chores involved in daily journalism. To have a chance to succeed at our larger goals, we must de-vote ourselves to the details of our craft. We must shun tricks and embrace thorough research. Then we must exercise our skills of writing and editing to present the information to the reader in a clear and useful way.

Devotion to detail will keep us closest to our more worthy ambitions. Journalism is a craft that calls for care and compe-tence. It starts with reporting, which should start with a com-mitment to truly understanding before trying to tell.

ABOUT THE AUTHOR

Terence Patrick Murphy was born March 3, 1936, at Sedalia, Missouri. He escaped at a tender age to the great State of Kansas, his forebears' home, where he was reared and educated in public schools at Topeka and Manhattan. Friends who kept track of his academic progress suggested that he go to barber's school ("We will always need barbers."). Uncle Sam said, "We will always need infantrymen" and sent him to Korea where he worked for the military newspaper, *Stars & Stripes*. After the Army, Murphy returned home and married Joan Sue Baldwin. In 1963, nine years after starting college, he was graduated from the University of Kansas at Lawrence, with a B.S. in journalism. His first journalism job was stringing high school sports at the age of sixteen. He has reported for United Press International, and edited for *The Akron Beacon-Journal* and *The Cincinnati Post*.

Upon graduation, he worked nine years for Harris newspapers in Kansas and Iowa. He spent nearly three years in the Harris management intern program at Ottawa, Kansas; Burlington, Iowa, and Spencer, Iowa; and was editor of the *Chanute Tribune* in Kansas from June 1968 to June 1972. He wrote this book while working as an assistant city editor for the *Minneapolis Tribune*.